Saxons vs. Vikings

Saxons vs. Vikings

Alfred the Great and England in the Dark Ages

Ed West

Skyhorse Publishing

Skyhorse Publishing books may be purchased in bulk at special discounts for sales promotion, corporate gifts, fund-raising, or educational purposes. Special editions can also be created to specifications. For details, contact the Special Sales Department, Skyhorse Publishing, 307 West 36th Street, 11th Floor, New York, NY 10018 or info@skyhorsepublishing.com.

Skyhorse® and Skyhorse Publishing® are registered trademarks of Skyhorse Publishing, Inc.®, a Delaware corporation.

Visit our website at www.skyhorsepublishing.com.

10 9 8 7 6 5 4 3 2 1

Library of Congress Cataloging-in-Publication Data is available on file.

Cover design by Rain Saukas

Paperback ISBN: 978-1-5107-7360-8
Hardcover ISBN: 978-1-5107-1985-9
Ebook ISBN: 978-1-5107-1990-3

Printed in the United States of America

Contents

Introduction

The Vikings first set foot in England in the year 787 near Portland on the south coast, in what was then the kingdom of Wessex. As they came ashore, a local official called Beaduheard walked up to their leader and explained that under government regulations they had to pay docking duties. The chief Viking put an axe through his head. Or, as the *Anglo-Saxon Chronicle* reported, "the reeve rode thither and tried to compel them to go to the royal manor, for he did not know what they were; and then they slew him."[1] Community relations were off to a tricky start.

It was the first of many such cultural misunderstandings: six years later, the Vikings attacked the holy island of Lindisfarne in the northern kingdom of Northumbria, killing a number of monks and taking the others off to a presumably grim life of slavery. The Lindisfarne massacre took place on June 8, 793, the feast day of Medard, patron saint of toothaches and the weather, and followed some bad omens of comets, whirlwinds, and fiery dragons seen in the sky. It was said in Europe that bad weather on St. Medard's Day would result in weeks of the same, so it was considered a terrible omen for the heathens to attack; worse still, earlier in 793, people in York had seen blood dripping from the roof of St. Peter's church.

The Portland reeve and his new Viking friends, who were probably from Horthaland or Hardanger Ford in Norway, would have been able to understand each other because the Anglo-Saxons were themselves pagan invaders from Scandinavia only three and a half centuries earlier, and the native Britons had then viewed their arrival with a similar lack of enthusiasm.

Although the Vikings soon disappeared from the coast of England for a few decades, the raiders returned in the 830s and the number of attacks increased as the ninth century dragged on, so that by the year 871 three of England's four kingdoms had been conquered; the last, Wessex, was poised to collapse as large Danish armies overwhelmed far smaller and less organized groups of natives. It was at this point that fate pushed forward a man who would shape an entire nation's history.

England may have never come to exist were it not for this one man, and it is with good reason that Alfred is the only English king to be known as "the Great."[2] He fought off the Danes; he unified England (well, sort of); he helped found a common law for everyone; he built towns for the first time since the Romans left; he introduced a navy; and most of all, he encouraged education and the arts in a country just emerging from centuries of illiteracy. Having learned to read in adulthood, King Alfred personally translated Latin texts into English and was the only king to write anything before Henry VIII, and the only European ruler between the second and thirteenth centuries to write on the philosophy of kingship.[3]

What's more surprising is that Alfred, the fifth and youngest son of King Ethelwulf, was a sickly and neurotic individual who comes across almost as a Woody Allen figure thrown into the horror of early medieval battle, forced to flee from these marauding Nordic maniacs. As he wrote much later in his translation of the Roman book *On the Consolation of Philosophy*, "the greatness of this earthly power never will please me, nor did I altogether very much yearn after this earthly authority." He would much rather have been a scholar stuck in a monastery reading the Bible and making beer.

After coming to the throne, Alfred would spend the next seven years on the run, eventually living out in a swamp, and on several occasions was almost captured—and considering that two of the other English kings in the past decade had been tortured to death, it was not an attractive prospect. He also had an extremely painful chronic stomach condition throughout his adult life, as if life wasn't terrible enough. Yet by the time he died, in 899, Wessex was safe, half of the neighboring kingdom of Mercia had been taken back from the Vikings, the derelict Roman city of London was rebuilt, and Alfred's family were well on the way to conquering all of England. His grandson Athelstan would finish the job twenty-eight years later, uniting the country under borders that remain roughly the same today. By the end of the millennium, "Englalond" was perhaps the most sophisticated society in western Europe, with the currency it still has today, the beginnings of a jury system, and a flourishing, highly literate Church.

It was a far cry from its origins a few centuries earlier, during a period usually called the Dark Ages.

CHAPTER ONE

Rome Answers the Prayers of the Britons. No, Says Rome

" The groans of the Britons . . . The barbarians drive us to the sea, the sea drives us to the barbarians; between these two means of death, we are either killed or drowned." So wrote the leaders of the province of Britannia in their final appeal to the Romans around the middle of the fifth century.

This message was recorded by Gildas, a depressive sixth-century British monk who chronicled the collapse of the country in his rather downbeat book (as hinted at by its title) *The Ruin and Conquest of Britain*. The barbarians he spoke of were raiders from across the North Sea, whom Gildas would have called *Saesneg* or *Garman* (Germans) but have become known to us as Anglo-Saxons. The first chapter in the history of England begins with these invaders who, three and a half-centuries later, faced the same fate themselves at the hands of a new wave of scary barbarians.

The story behind the Saxon and Viking invasions is told in *The Anglo-Saxon Chronicle*, one of two works commissioned by King Alfred in the ninth century, the other being a biography written by a Welsh monk called Asser. Both books painted Alfred rather heroically, but even taking aside any bias, we know that when he came to power Anglo-Saxon England was almost finished, and when he died Alfred had established a dynasty whose descendants still rule England today. In creating laws and in bringing the country under the influence of the Latin cultural world, he also set the ground for the English political and legal system.

Asser was a Welsh monk hired by Alfred during a relatively peaceful period of his rule, which was otherwise mainly characterized by Viking attacks. Asser's biography begins in the biblical style by explaining the king's descent: Alfred was the son of King Ethelwulf of Wessex, who was son of King Egbert, and so on, going back to the earliest rulers of the kingdom, a line which starts with the semi-mythical Cerdic in the sixth century. Cerdic, although his existence is somewhat doubted, was said to be the founder of the Kingdom of the West Saxons, sailing over from Germany and arriving in Hampshire in 495. Through Cerdic, Asser traced Alfred's line back to Woden and Geat and various other mythical Germanic figures on the continent, before the family tree inexplicably joins up to the Biblical line of Seth and Noah and all the way back to Adam.

The Angles and Saxons who conquered most of what was then the Roman province of Britannia were illiterate, and so their earliest history was recorded by their enemies and victims, the Britons, who unsurprisingly did not give them a very good press. Gildas described the arrival of the Saxons as being like "a pack of cubs" followed by "a larger troop of satellite dogs." The words of help he recalled about the groans of the Britons were sent probably in AD 449 to Agitius, consul of Rome, in an appeal for help against the barbarian invaders. The Romans answered their prayers. But unfortunately the answer was "no," or more precisely "look after your own affairs."

Writing in the following century, and from the relative safety of Armorica, where many Britons had fled (which is why it is now called Brittany, and has among the highest rates of alcoholism in France),

Gildas penned his book, which curses not just the Saxons but the various rulers who had brought disaster on Britain. Among these are Constantine, "the tyrannical whelp of the unclean lioness of Damnonia," "thou bear" Cuneglasse, whoever he was, and another, Maglocune, who he calls the "dragon of the island." Gildas wrote how "the first wave landed on the eastern side of the island . . . and there they fixed their terrible claws, as if to defend the country, but in fact to attack it. Their German mother-land, seeing them successfully installed, dispatched a wonderful collection of hangers-on and dogs, who, arriving by the boatload, joined up with their misbegotten comrades." He also quoted liberally from the *Book of Revelations*, the Biblical book of choice for all lunatics down the ages,[4] and his prose sometimes gets a little heated. Gildas was a sort of proto-doom-mongering newspaper columnist predicting everything was going to the dogs; and of course, he was completely right— Britain was doomed.

It was a hardly the best of times for anyone. The map of Europe at the end of the fourth century resembles a chaotic weather chart, full of arrows that record the movements of various tribes making their way across the continent in enormous war bands of up to 80,000 people. The Vandals came from what is now Poland and travelled to Germany, then France and down to Spain, before crossing over to Tunisia and then to Sicily, eventually sacking Rome in 455; their name survives in Andalucía (and for someone who mindlessly smashes things up, although by most accounts they weren't the worst). The Visigoths started out in Romania and invaded Greece before landing in southern Italy and going up and down the entire length of the country and then settling in central Spain, where they ruled for several centuries, abandoning paganism and becoming enthusiastically intolerant Christians. And while the Black Sea was being raided by Goths and Heruls from Scandinavia as far back as the third century, the northern shore of the European empire in what is now Belgium was attacked by a "confederation of many tribes" that called themselves the Franks. The Romans eventually regained control, and both sides of the English Channel were put under a military command who built what are called Saxon Shore-forts, most likely by employing barbarians from Saxony to protect the region; eventually large numbers of Saxons were used to defend Britain from other alarming long-haired Germans.

However, the Huns were the most adventurous, and terrifying, of the barbarians, originating in central Asia and travelling across the vast steppes of Russia before reaching Transylvania, where they split up, one group arriving somewhere near Paris and the other invading Italy. Even the sort of grunting, hairy-faced Goths and Vandals who gave Romans sleepless nights were themselves terrified of the Huns, who had introduced the stirrups from central Asia and so vastly increased the area horsemen could cross. This only encouraged further Germanic expansion into Roman territory, as generally the Huns didn't make very good neighbors.

Why was Rome collapsing? There were a number of reasons, but the decline was so slow and the argument so controversial you could write a six-volume book about it. The empire had problems with inflation, it had problems with powerful generals starting civil wars, it had a massive problem with birth rates, and with the barbarian tribes on its doorstep, who had become too numerous to deal with.

Bit by bit distant parts of the western empire began to be settled by Germans, with the Romans no longer having the strength to oppose them. Now what the Britons found was that top of the "what the Romans did for us" list was "security." To the north, the Picts, distantly related to the Britons, though not close enough to be invited over for Christmas, had been kept out for four centuries by the Roman army stationed on Hadrian's Wall. But with the imperial army gone, they began raiding and pillaging from their Caledonian homeland into what had been the province of Britannia. The Britons asked the imperial army to help them, but Emperor

Honorius had his own problems, as the Visigoths had just sacked Rome and kidnapped his aunt.

And while Romans cried laments about the ruin of their crops and the slaughter of their families, other people had to deal with climate change as well. At the very north of Germany was the region of Angeln, the "thin peninsula," low lying and prone to floods, and unfortunately during this period there was a rise in temperatures called the Little Climatic Optimum; tribes in the Low Countries tried to get around the problem by building their homes on artificial mounds, but eventually even they fled.

To the south of Angeln lived the Saxons, named after the *scramaseax*, a type of battle knife they used, and to the north the Jutes; all three tribes (we can guess) faced population pressure at home that made crossing the freezing North Sea to fight Caledonians seem like an attractive prospect. And luckily the collapse of Western civilization brought with it certain job opportunities in what we'd now call the security industry.

Unable to defend themselves from the maniacs on their border, the British leaders decided that the best way to get rid of scary barbarians was to hire other scary barbarians to fight them—German mercenaries from Angeln. A foolproof plan, and one that made sense at the time; the Romans had been using Saxons as hired muscle for centuries, so they were thought to be hardworking, trustworthy, and, best of all, very cheap. They were the first economic migrants hired to do work that the natives wouldn't do themselves.

There had been a large German community in Norfolk as far as back as AD 320, while Germans of various sorts had been fighting in the Roman army in Britain for far longer, although not with entirely successful results. One of the first mention of Germans on the island dates from AD 83, when some conscripts murdered their commanding officer and other regular soldiers, stole three ships, and tried to sail home around Scotland. They were shipwrecked along the way and reduced to eating each other, and when the survivors got home to the Rhineland they were kidnapped by their own people and sold as slaves—to the Romans. How they must have laughed at the irony.

Once the Romans left, the Britons also descended into fighting among themselves, and a series of king-warlords emerged, some of whose names have survived in legend, among them Old King Cole. Cole, or Coel Hen, may have been a Roman general-turned-usurper (there were plenty of these around) or a native Briton ruling the area known as Hen Ogledd in Welsh, "old north"—that is, northern England and southern Scotland. How a barely historical king living in the fifth century ended up as a popular nursery rhyme in the early eighteenth century is a bit of a mystery, but it was certainly around in Welsh by around 1200.

About a century later, a far more influential figure called Wyrtgeorn or Vortigen emerged, although "Vortigen" most likely just means "king"; his full title, according to Gildas, was "Vortigen of the repulsive mouth." Gildas wasn't a fan.

Vortigen's handling of these admittedly challenging times seems to have fallen short of ideal; either in AD 430 or 449 he hired three boatloads of poor, hungry, and violent Jutes, led by two brothers called Horsa and Hengest, "the Horse and the Stallion," to fight the Picts. The mercenaries arrived in the former Roman province of Cantium and brought with them some of their women folk, including Hengest's daughter Rowena, said to be a great beauty (or at least by the standards of the Dark Ages, which presumably weren't very high). According to legend, Vortigen fell in love with the girl and offered the Jutes the Isle of Thanet (then with the far more Welsh sounding name Ynys Ruym) if he could win her heart. The tough guys did their job, Vortigen got his girl, and the Jutes were given the small island. (It should be noted for the sake of pedants that this story is probably entirely fictitious, in fact almost certainly so.)

The next time the Jutes returned with twenty boats, and soon after with sixty. At this point, some of the more pessimistic natives must have wondered if they weren't a bit overstaffed on the mercenary front, and whether in fact something slightly sinister might be going on. Vortigen told the Germans they were no longer needed and to go elsewhere, refusing to pay them anymore; the Jutes now rebelled and overran the whole of Cantium, or Kent as they called it, and, to make things worse, the Picts joined up with the same people who had been paid to attack them.

According to legend, the Jutes and Britons agreed to meet for peace talks, with 300 unarmed men on each side, but before any sort of road map for peace could be laid out, Hengest and his men took out their concealed daggers and massacred all the Britons, except (conveniently) Vortigen. The talks were therefore concluded. Presumably this was how Vortigen explained the story, which became known as the Treachery of the Long Knives, when he later turned up in Wales, and since the Jutes were incapable of telling their side of the story, we'll never know.

The Saxons, who had been doing similar work further up the North Sea coast, arrived in force and took the land on the other side of the Thames Estuary, now called "the Kingdom of the east Saxons," or Essex. Further north still the Angles arrived in areas that would become known as East Anglia, Lincolnshire, Yorkshire, and Northumberland.

Even the most liberal cultural relativist of the fifth century, if there was such a thing, must have seen the new state of affairs as a backwards step. The Romano-British lived in cities, could read and write, visited public baths, enjoyed the theatre, spoke Latin, and drank imported wine. The Britons were civilized, and tried to ignore the invaders like one would ignore a maniac causing a scene on public transport—by giving him money in the hope he would go away.

Gildas, who really didn't appreciate the cultural diversity that the Anglo-Saxons had introduced to his country, calling them "bloodthirsty, proud, parricidal, warlike and adulterous enemies of God," described how the Britons gave the *Garmans* food at first "to shut the dog's mouth" (he was not very keen on dogs either), but each concession was met with fresh demands for land. Of course no extortionist in history has ever simply left his victim alone as long as they paid out, and the Anglo-Saxons were no different.

The Saxons were not urban sophisticates; they had the front of their heads shaved and hair grown long at the back in order to make their faces look larger and scarier,[5] and they may have practiced human sacrifice, and possibly drank from the skulls of their enemies. Sidonius Apollinaris, a Roman chronicler of the fifth century wrote that "the Saxon surpasses all others in brutality,"[6] and presumably there was a lot of competition at the time. According to the Roman historian Tacitus, the Saxons also used to crucify or drown one in ten prisoners.

The invaders only bothered to occupy three Roman sites: Lincoln, Bath, and Cirencester, although they also built a new settlement a mile west of Roman Londonium called Lundenwic. The vast majority settled in small villages, and, following the Saxon conquest, most of the Roman cities were deserted, which romantic Victorian historians liked to put down to their ancestors' earthy, honest manliness but was more likely because they didn't know how to operate things like plumbing. The Angles and Saxons also possibly avoided the Roman ruins as they thought them haunted, and built by giants,[7] and Gildas said, in ever cheery fashion, that "the cities of our country are still not inhabited as they were; even today they are squalid deserted ruins." (Gildas could be quite depressing sometimes.)

Unlike the Romans, they weren't great road builders, and it wasn't until the eighteenth century that any improvements were made on English highways. Their method of architecture—building one-story homes out of pig dung—rather contrasts with the glories that were Roman architecture, and their most lasting physical legacy was the series of great big chalk pictures in the ground, the most famous being the White Horse of Uffington. Impressive though this is, it's hardly the Coliseum.

Out also went the rich variety of food that came with being part of a large empire, such as whole roasted boar downed with figs and Italian wine consumed while inside a heated dining room while boys in togas read from Homer; in came porridge, which is what the Anglo-Saxon diet consisted almost entirely of at the time, eaten inside dung-houses.

It's always said of the British that they're slow to rouse, but that eventually they'll face the enemy and beat them. Unfortunately, the Ancient Britons didn't have the Americans on their side or, to use that common historical comparison, Rome. And so as the simple employer/tradesman relationship deteriorated into outright hostility, the Britons were overwhelmed by people Gildas described as "hated by God and men alike."

Again they appealed to Rome. The Romans didn't even bother replying this time; the old empire was but a shell of its former glory, in retreat on all sides. It was like radio silence in the disaster movie where the people out in the cabin realize they're all alone.

Instead the Latin-speaking British elite did what all defeated people do and headed for higher ground, or across the sea to Armorica, which became known as Brittany, or "Lesser Britain" (which is why Britain is "Great Britain"). Most of the population stayed behind to live under Saxon rule and to eventually adopt their language. It must have seemed like the end of civilization for many—but still, at least they got rid of the Picts.

The Britons called the invaders the *Saesneg*, as the English are today called by their neighbors to the west (in Scottish Gaelic it is *Sassenach* and in Cornish *Sowsnek*). They in turn referred to the natives as *Welsh*, which has a variety of meanings but none of them particularly positive, either "slave," "foreigner" or "dark stranger" (likewise the French-speaking Belgians are called Walloons and Wallachia in Romania has the same etymology, while Cornwall, Walsall, and Walthamstow in London probably all come from *Wal*).

The Welsh, or Cymraeg, referred to the neighboring country as "Lloegyr," literally "the lost lands."

The Germans themselves would eventually call their new homeland *Angelcyn*, or as it was known by the turn of the millennium, *Englalond*.

CHAPTER TWO

The Tattooed People

The name Britain was almost certainly coined by Pytheas, a Greek sailor from Marseilles, who in 330 BC sailed all the way to northern Scotland on a hunch. The Phoenicians, who came from what is now Lebanon, had long been aware of the island, as had the Greeks (the fifth century BC historian Herodotus referred to the Cassiterides, or Tin Islands)[8] but no one knew exactly where they were and Pytheas was the first to actually make the insanely risky journey.

Not that he got any credit for his great efforts; Pytheas came back from his trip telling of lands where the sun shone only two hours a day, a place so cold that men lived in log cabins, and of giant sea animals that sprayed water from their heads. Unaccustomed to the sight of whales or the joys of Scottish winters, everyone just thought he was talking the sort of old sea dog rubbish sailors usually come up with.

When they arrived about eight centuries later the Anglo-Saxons were, according to best estimates, the tenth group to make a large-scale crossing to the island.

The oldest human remains in Britain are 30,000 years old, and belong to the Red Lady of Paviland, who was actually a man; the skeleton was discovered by a nineteenth-century religious fundamentalist, who thinking the world only 6,000 years old assumed by its red dye that it must have belonged to a Roman prostitute. During the last ice age humans left the island, which was at that point joined to the continent because sea levels were so high, and only returned about 11,000 years ago; the second oldest skeleton, Cheddar Gorge Man, dates to around 7150 BC and was discovered at the start of the nineteenth century inside Britain's biggest cave. (Curiously enough, in 1996 scientists found a direct match in the female line to Cheddar Man living only a few miles away in Bristol, a forty-two-year-old history teacher called Adrian who carried the same mitochondrial DNA, so his mother's mother's mother etc. descended from Cheddar Man's mother's mother's mother.)

Cheddar Man's life had ended in his mid-twenties, when someone smashed his head in, and documented evidence suggests that this probably wasn't that unusual in prehistoric Britain. At the time one in fifty could expect to die from being hit over the head with a club, and one in thirteen suffered a similar attack at some point in their life. These statistics, based on the skulls of those people unlucky to live between 4000 and 3200 BC, only include head wounds—it is also likely that the natives used deer antlers to stab each other to death. In retrospect Gildas had nothing to complain about.

About nine separate waves of people crossed the Channel before the Romans, with agriculture first arriving around 3700 BC, and a big change in technology coming near 2000 BC with the so-called "Beaker People" (they built beakers, as can be guessed by the name). Bronze Age Britain, which lasted from 2500 BC to approximately 800 BC, when the Iron Age kicks in, was not much better than the Stone Age in terms of life quality, in fact probably worse;[9] several sites across the country have shown evidence of massacres, one of the grisliest (and therefore most fascinating to archaeologists) being Fin Top in the Peak District, where lots of people were killed together in what was probably some grim *Apocalypto*-style slaughter. DNA research suggests the natives were related in some way to the Basques of northwest Spain, whose baffling language is totally unconnected to any other in Europe, being a survivor of the indigenous languages that were almost entirely replaced by Indo-European speakers between 4000–1000 BC, and in Britain later.[10] Apart from Hungarian, Finnish, and Estonian, all other European languages are at least vaguely related in that they're part of the Indo-European group. In Britain the Indo-European invaders were called the Celts, who must have been in charge after they arrived because everyone ended up speaking their language.

But despite Cheddar Man's language being lost, we know that the pre-Celtic invaders gave us two of the two oldest words in English— Thames and Clyde—although we don't know which invaders, as there were several waves of people, some up the coast of Iberia and France and others from across the North Sea.

The major legacy of ancient Britain is Stonehenge, which was completed around 2600 BC, and though it is possibly a sun dial (or possibly a burial site), it seems strangely ambitious; the proto-Britons had yet to domesticate horses, yet they were prepared to drag enormous stones 250 miles from Wales to Wiltshire to build this enormous monument. It would be as if Haiti suddenly announced it was sending a man to Mars. Rather unsurprisingly, Stonehenge took 3,000 years to build and must have been a constant source of grumbling for those forced to help out. Their second most impressive surviving monument was a small wooden dresser also discovered in Wiltshire.

By Pytheas's day the island was dominated by Celts, Iron Age people who had migrated across central Europe (although there is a confusion over the name, and whether the Celts of Britain and France were related to the Celts of Austria. The confusion arises because the Romans called any Barbarians who weren't obviously German "Celts"). These Ancient Britons had crossed the channel between 900 and 500 BC in two waves, and spoke a Brythonic language that was the ancestor of Welsh. It was the their fondness for tattoos that earned the island the name Pretani, or Britain—land of the tattooed people.[11] Another word for the country—Albion—came from the Celtic word for white, after the White Cliffs of Dover (Alps also has the same origin).[12]

We don't know too much about the Celts either, although compared to the original inhabitants they were probably the height of sophistication. They divided themselves into about twenty tribes, and the most powerful of their kings, a man called Cunobelinus but turned into Cymbeline in the Shakespeare's play, founded the first city, Catuvellauni (Colchester).

They certainly weren't noble savages. The Romans called the more sophisticated Celts of northern Gaul and southeast Britain the Belgae, and they were known to be able to read and write (when the Dutch and French agreed to create a country because they couldn't bear to share a border, they called it after the tribe). Though they had no native literature or major art, the Belgae left some nice mementos to their society—at Park Street farmstead in Hertfordshire earthworks turned up iron shackles used for a chain gang while, more sinister, the discovery of ninety-seven babies at Hambleden in Buckinghamshire suggests unwanted female newborns discarded from a slave farm.

And thanks to forensic research we do know that they took magic mushrooms, and so we can only imagine the shock they got when the Emperor Claudius turned up on the back of an elephant in AD 44.

The Romans believed, like all people who were aware of the place, that the native population of Britain practiced human sacrifices and had one eye. Who knows where the one eye myth came from—maybe they met one, and just assumed they all had the same problem—but they were possibly right about the other thing. Various mass burial sites suggest a country not unacquainted with extreme violence, but as for written evidence we only have the Romans' word for it. In fact one gets the impression that generally speaking the Britons disgusted the Romans, as suggested by their term for them, *Brittunculi*—wretched little Brits. Despite their love of gladiatorial gore, the Romans hated human sacrifice and held in contempt any group who practiced it; while they also saw tattoos as a mark of criminality and slavery, and used it both as a punishment and a form of branding.

In the second and early first century BC Rome went through a period of massive expansion, and in 58 BC General Julius Caesar overran Gaul (today's France), killing about a million natives, according to Roman sources (Romans tended to play up how many civilians they killed in conquering a country, which only demonstrated how awesome they were). Northern Gaul was inhabited by troublesome Belgae tribes with close cultural and trading links with southeast Britain, so any native with a good understanding of geopolitical theory would have seen what was coming next. Although it's fair to say there probably weren't many around.

Caesar, with the sort of egotism that stood out even in Rome, and with ambition that would either make him master of the world or get him killed (the latter, as it turned out), soon began planning his next conquest. With an invasion in mind, he sent over a tame Belgic king from northern Gaul called Commius to persuade the natives about the benefits of not resisting the Romans. Commius had claimed to be a well-respected and influential man around the southeast, but he was seized almost as soon as he landed, and ended up as a hostage.

Not easily put off, in 55 BC Caesar arrived with 10,000 men in the kingdom of Cantium, home of the Cantiaci tribe and preserved in the names Kent and Canterbury. He landed close to what is now Dover, and after impressing the natives with his enormous army, left; the locals had tracked the Roman ships on chariots, making it perfectly clear, through the universal language of violence, that the newcomers weren't welcome. The following year Caesar actually landed with a far bigger army, didn't like the weather, and went back to Rome again to celebrate with a record twenty-day triumphant feast; five days longer for a day trip to Dover than the one he received for conquering all of France.

Four years later Rome descended into civil war, Caesar was murdered, and for the next one hundred years the Empire was content to trade with the Britons rather than endure the hassle of conquering them. Besides the effort involved, even the most sophisticated Roman felt uneasy about crossing the sea to a land populated with flesh-eating cyclopses. Some Romans crash landed in Britain in AD 16, where they were apparently well treated by the locals, but still came back full of stories about the place being full of monsters.

The half-insane Emperor Caligula tried to land in AD 39 or 40, but screwed it up, and was soon murdered, but four years later his successor and uncle Claudius launched an invasion. The pretext was Druidism, a Celtic cult that flourished in Gaul and Britain. We tend to think of Druids as harmless cranks messing around with magic potions, but their ritualistic religious murders gave the Romans their moral excuse, and besides which the Gaulish Druids were receiving help from their friends across the water. (Again, this is from Roman sources, who weren't entirely impartial observers of native culture.) Add to this an invitation from one British tribe for assistance, and an emperor with a crippled leg and a speech impediment who was very keen not to get murdered, and it's no surprise that the Romans invaded in AD 43.

A force of 40,000 men under Aulus Plautius assembled at Boulogne, but things got off to a blundering start when the soldiers mutinied, afraid about going over the ocean. Claudius ordered his minister Narcissus to reason with them; Narcissus was an ex-slave (in Roman society educated freed men could climb very high up the social ladder) and sending him may have further infuriated the proud legionaries, but instead they were amused that this lowly servant was telling them what to do, and cheered "Io (pronounced Yo) Saturnalia," a reference to the strange annual Roman festival where slaves would wear their masters' clothes.[13]

Maybe out of fear, or perhaps just shyness, the Britons ignored the Roman invasion at first. But after wandering around Kent for several days, the Romans managed to pick a fight on the Medway river, where the Second legion engaged the Belgic tribes in battle. After a day's combat proved inconclusive, the two sides agreed to go back to base and resume in the morning—a quite sporting way to do battle. The Romans won the second day's play, crossed the Thames, and took the whole southeast.

Claudius completed the victory by marching into Catuvellauni on an elephant, deliberately chosen to impress on the natives how powerful their visitors were. He renamed the city Camulodunum, installed it as the capital of the province of Britannia, and had a great big statue of himself built in its center, designed to make him look like his more manly relative Julius Caesar. He then erected an arch back in Rome, proclaiming that he had beaten eleven kings (albeit tiny ones). The Colchester statue disappeared when the Romans fled and the region was flooded four centuries later, only to turn up in 1907 when a boy swimming in the River Alde in Suffolk found it. And even though the Romans had only conquered southern Britain, their reputation spread so far that even the chief of the distant Orkneys sent an ambassador to proclaim his loyalty.

Not that they were entirely welcome; Caractacus of the Catuvellauni tribe led an armed resistance in the west, before taking refuge with the northern Brigantes. But the Brigantes' queen Cartumandua sided with the Romans and handed him over, and Caractacus was forced to walk through the city of Rome in the triumphal parade before facing execution, after first being presented as a barbarian curiosity to the Senate. However Caractacus explained to the Senate that his stubborn bloody resistance only proved just how glorious Rome was, and that only the greatest nation on earth could have conquered his army and that, furthermore, only the greatest nation on earth would set him free as an example of just how great they were, and give him a nice cushy job and a house. This is how the Roman historian Tacitus, who was famous for putting great speeches into the mouths of illiterate barbarians, recorded it: 'If I were now being handed over as one who had surrendered immediately, neither my fortune nor your glory would have achieved brilliance. It is also true that in my case any reprisal will be followed by oblivion. On the other hand, if you preserve me safe and sound, I shall be an eternal example of your clemency.'

However he expressed it, the Senate freed him. Caractacus became an overnight sensation and spent the rest of his life as a local celebrity in the imperial capital.

But Cartumandua's ex-husband Venutius, bitter because she had humiliated him by leaving him for his armor-bearer, began a rebellion largely out of spite to his ex-wife; it ended up as a nationwide revolt, with the Brigantes queen being kicked out by her own people. Eventually the Romans put it down, and though Venutius's punishment is unrecorded, it was most likely something gruesome.

Though there followed two decades of relative peace in the new province, a far more dangerous rebellion then erupted, largely over land, inheritance tax, and cultural misunderstandings about the role of women. The Iceni tribe of what is now Norfolk were allies of the Romans until their king Prasutagus died in AD 60. As was the custom, Prasutagus left half his possessions to the Roman Emperor, the truly and utterly mad Nero, while the other half of his estate went to his wife Boudicca. This was the Celtic tradition, but for the macho Romans it was unthinkable that a woman, and especially a barbarian woman, should inherit such a land when it was their custom that conquered rulers hand over all of their territory to the emperor. After taking Boudicca's estate and having her whipped, the local Roman officials raped her two daughters.

At the time the main Roman army, led by Governor Suetonius Paullinus, was on the River Dee in what is now Wales, facing a strange sight that must have confirmed all their worst prejudices about the natives: long-haired harridans dressed entirely in black and looking like hellish figures from Roman mythology, waving torches about while behind them stood the Druids, with uplifted arms, shouting magic curses and pouring the blood of Roman prisoners onto their sacred groves. It was the ultimate clash of cultures: the new-age free spirits of Celtic mysticism vs. the short back and sides squares of the Roman imperial army. It meant that the Governor was not around to handle the delicate diplomatic situation among the Iceni.

As it was, the treatment of Boudicca's daughters (she became known as Boudicea only through a sixteenth-century spelling error) sparked a violent revolt by the Iceni, which quickly spread as neighboring tribes joined her cause. As well as the mistreatment of the Iceni ruling family, the Britons had all sorts of other gripes against the Romans, including the confiscation of native lands, and the taxes they had to pay for the imperial cult; not only did they have to give money to the emperor, and worship him as a god, but they had to pay taxes to worship him as a god.

Boudicca sacked three cities in quick succession. Such was their total surprise of the revolt that the Romans hadn't even built proper walls around Camulodunum, and the entire population was massacred. The worst attack was on Londonium, which had first been established in AD 47[14]: today there is a layer of red ash five feet underneath the city, remnants of the fire caused by Boudicca's army, somewhere between the decaying tube tunnels and the square mile's post-ironic office blocks. The molten glass discovered points to temperatures reaching 1000 degrees after the sacking of Londonium, similar to that of the firebombing of Dresden in February 1945.

Altogether 70,000 people were burned, stabbed, or crucified in Colchester, London and Verulamium (now St. Alban's)—not a single person is said to have survived the sackings, according to (obviously biased) Roman accounts. Roman opinion was horrified by the tales that spread across the channel of heinous atrocities, the historians focusing rather unnecessarily on the indignities committed against women. Romans were perennially terrified of uprisings by slaves and barbarians, although you could argue, and these stories turned them hysterical.

It got worse. Along the way her army met the Roman Legion IX and cut them to pieces, killing 2,000 soldiers. Panic gripped the empire, and such was the terror in Britannia that the legionary in charge of the southwest, Poenius Postumus, refused to march on the rebel army.

But having given the Druids a slaying, the Governor's crack Roman army now marched all the way to the southeast. Suetonius' band was too small to save London or St. Albans, but as he raised more men along the way his troops followed the rebels up Watling Street, the main Roman road that linked London to Chester.

"I am fighting for my lost freedom, my bruised body and my outraged daughters. Consider how many of you are fighting and why—then you will win this battle, or perish! That is what I, a woman, plan to do! Let the men live in slavery if they want to." With these stirring words, she led thousands of her countrymen to be slaughtered at the Battle of Watling Street. (This is how the Roman Tacitus recorded events, although whether she actually came up with such eloquence is open to debate.)

Despite the Romans still numbering only 10,000, and the Britons up to 230,000 (again, without weighing you down with caveats, any figure from the ancient world should be treated with massive skepticism), the ensuing battle was only going one way. The Romans camped in a gorge with a forest behind them, ensuring that only a small number of natives could attack them at any one time, a battle plan similar in principle to that of villains in kung-fu movies coming at the hero one by one rather than just overwhelming him. In contrast to the *Braveheart*-style appeals of Boudicca to her people, Suetonius told his men, presumably in a posh accent sounding like Charles Dance: "Ignore the racket made by these savages. There are more women than men in their ranks. They are not soldiers—they're not even properly equipped. We've beaten them before and when they see our weapons and feel our spirit, they'll crack." The Romans unleashed a volley of *pila*, their custom-made javelins which bent on impact, and so could neither be returned nor pulled out of a now useless shield.

But as well as having little armor and holding a bad position, the Britons made a further mistake; it was their custom to bring along their women and children to watch the battles from the sidelines, a practice that must have kept child psychologists in work for years. Like some awful holiday traffic jam, the civilians' wagons blocked the way of the soldiers trying to retreat, and by the end of the day 80,000 Britons were dead—against just 400 Romans. After news of the victory spread the cowardly Postumus did the honourable thing and stabbed himself to death, while poor old Suetonius was sacked, and replaced with a more hearts and minds-style governor. It was like one of those FBI/CIA dramas where the bureaucracy always punished the hero for his success.

Boudicca probably swallowed poison rather than face capture and crucifixion, and legend had it that she is buried under King's Cross Station—platform nine, to be precise—although evidence suggesting the battle was somewhere in the midlands sort of refutes this nice story.

It's lucky that Boudicca is even remembered. The one record of this uprising, Tacitus's history of Britain, was soon lost and only rediscovered in Tudor times, when Boudicca soon became a cult figure. Elizabeth I, a fiery, red-headed queen of Welsh ancestry engaged in war with the Spanish, was obviously keen on encouraging her subjects to honour another ginger firebrand who fought a bunch of Latins (although there is no record that Boudicca had red hair). And so the Iceni warrior, once forgotten, became a powerful symbol of British courage and independence.[15]

The empire was shaken by the rebellion of the wretched little Brits and Nero wanted to leave the island altogether. But the

Romans weren't the type of people to sit around gazing at their shoes or holding peace rallies: only twenty years later they marched into Caledonia where, in another ludicrously one-sided battle, they slaughtered 10,000 natives with only 360 Roman losses.

Within five years things had calmed down enough for the Romans to withdraw one of their legions, and Britain settled down to become a placid province from AD 78 under new governor Gnaeus Julius Agricola. The local aristocracy, given the choice of drinking Italian wine and hanging around spas reading poetry, or living in wooden huts, were soon Romanized. Agricola certainly got a good press, but then again the only historian of the period, Tacitus, happened to be his son-in-law.

Agricola made sure that the sons of leading Britons were educated in the Roman way, and within a generation many locals were wearing togas and speaking Latin. Roads were built, connecting new cities such as Lincoln, Chester, and Exeter, and each town had a market, town hall, public baths, gyms and saunas, an amphitheater, and temples.

Londonium seems to have become the capital around 100, although there were settlements in Greater London dating back millennia. The city attracted traders soon after its foundation, and the discovery of its first legal document around that time suggests that lawyers had infected it by the end of the century. It boasted its own forum (marketplace) and at its peak had 60,000 people, even after an enormous accidental fire destroyed it in 125 (big fires were fairly common in wooden Roman cities; St. Albans went the same way thirty years later). Lindum, or Lincoln, was established in AD 90, while Glevum—Gloucester—followed in around 96, originally as a retirement village for old Roman soldiers. The city arose as an indirect result of Boudicca's rebellion—to avoid arguments with the natives, the Romans built on land reclaimed from the sea.

Under Roman rule the population of Britain rose to about three million, a figure it wouldn't reach for another thousand years, and this included a fairly cosmopolitan population. There were Greeks in London, Lincoln, and Carlisle; Caledonians in Colchester; Gauls in Bath, Lincoln, and Cirencester; Germans in Monmouthshire; and Sardinians in York.

Being on the fringes, Britain required an enormous standing army compared to other provinces, some 50,000 strong, and the vast majority of soldiers were in the north of the province. About 10,000 of these northern troops were stationed on the famous wall, named after the emperor whose notable other claim was to introduce Greek-style beards and Greek attitudes towards homosexuality (he openly lived with his lover, Antonius, whose buff physique has been preserved for posterity thanks to various sculptures). In 122 AD Emperor Hadrian had decreed that the Empire's borders should be fixed and secure, and to do this in northern Britain required more than just a couple of flag poles and a humorless customs officer.

At its completion Hadrian's Wall was eighty miles along, eight feet thick, and fifteen feet high, with a fort every fifteen miles and a ditch on each side. But it was built not just to keep the barbarian Picts from Caledonia out, but to also keep two troublemaking British tribes apart, the Brigantes to the south and the Selgovae to the north. Whenever a rebellion was reported back at headquarters, one or both of their names would crop up, so the Romans decided to separate them altogether, like naughty schoolboys.

But the northern tribesmen continued to cause trouble. In 180 the Caledonians invaded Britannia and killed the Roman military leader. Replacement Ulpius Marcellus successfully beat the Picts, but was lucky to escape getting beaten to death by his own troops, who mutinied against his stern rule. Emperor Commodus, meanwhile, who hadn't had much to do with the victory, took the credit by renaming himself Britannicus. After Marcellus fled back to Rome, the soldiers then mutinied against his replacement Pertinax; the rebellion was crushed and Pertinax returned to Rome, where he ended up murdering Commodus in 193 and becoming emperor himself, only to be murdered soon after.[16] Politics was obviously quite complex.

By this stage the quality of Roman soldiering seemed to be on the decline—surveys of Hadrian's Wall show that most of the time half the men were absent or sick, and this despite having heated baths, toilets, a hospital, and a wide selection of food. The Romans began importing foreigners to police the country, including up to 5,500 horsemen from Sarmatia, in what is now Russia, and, more ominously, Saxons from Germany.

The very size of Britain's military made its administrators a source of anxiety in Rome; such was the paranoia that Emperor Domitian put to death one governor, Sallustius Lucullus, for naming a lance after himself. And it wasn't totally irrational—many of the Governors of Britannia did cause trouble. Constantinus, who was an Augustus, or deputy emperor, captured London in 296, and as a reward to the city renamed it Augusta, after himself. After his death at York ten years later, his son Constantine proclaimed himself emperor and forcibly took control of Rome.

The north had a different character to the more civilized, flatter south, and the Romans even had different words for the passive *Britanni* of the south and the trouble-making *Brittones* of the north. By the end of the empire life in Britannia Superior, the south, had become very Roman; there the natives used imported olive oil and ate Mediterranean fruit and vegetables, including new products like peas, turnips, cabbages, and parsnips, and their gardens now featured that quintessentially English flower, the rose. The southern Britons almost certainly spoke Latin in everyday life, while the northerners maintained their native languages. The Romans also introduced apples, turning the south of England into one big orchard, and also the domestic cat—in return Britain exported its famously vicious dogs.

The southern Britons even worshipped like Romans, often by combining their native deities with Latin ones. While the Romans, like the Greeks, believed in anthropomorphic gods who behaved like spoiled, sexually depraved playboys, the Celts worshipped nature—trees, rivers, and the spirits. But the imperialists never had any problem with foreign religions, and simply co-opted foreign gods and pasted them onto their own, a system that worked surprisingly well until they came across a group in Judea who had this crazy idea that there was only one god.

One example of this religious fusion can be found in the statues left buried all over Britain; while pre-Roman Celts would collect the heads of their enemies and keep them as shrines, the Romans worshipped that most obvious of fertility symbols, the phallus. They stumbled on a combination that most modern people would see as unflattering were it done to a bust of them.

The Britons really took to one aspect of Roman religion, the habit of writing curses on broken bits of pottery and leaving them at shrines, a lot of which have been recovered by diggings; usually they are requests for the gods to punish cheating wives or thieves. "By this Tacita is cursed and declared putrefied like rotting blood" is a typical example of a religious offering left by one embittered ex-boyfriend. What happened to Tacita or her ex we'll never know.

The upper classes, meanwhile, went in for the mystery religions, the pseudo-spiritual babble of late Roman civilization. Some of the mystery religions were sanitized versions of Egyptian paganism, others were orgiastic cults of Bacchus the booze god, while some took bits from various cults and jumbled them together. The current Bank of England in the City of London sits on top of one mystery temple.

But for city people, both rich and poor, there was an even more strange eastern religion, a small Jewish sect that quickly became fashionable. The Empire brought with it safe opportunities for trade and travel, allowing Christianity to spread all over the Mediterranean and beyond, and by AD 200 it had already established a foothold on the island. Britain's first martyr, St. Alban, died around AD 304 after he sheltered a Christian priest and was so impressed by his bravery that he willingly chose death over paganism. Brave though this was, had he hung on just nine years he would not have needed to make the sacrifice as the religion was legalized, although he wouldn't have had a Hertfordshire commuter town named after him.

In 313 Emperor Constantine the Great went into battle with the cross on his shield and thanked his new best friend—God—by allowing His people to practice their faith in freedom, in a better world where, pagan or Christian, people could be free to believe in what they wanted.

In 391 Emperor Theodosius had all the pagan temples closed and their shrines smashed up.

By now the Western Empire was in terminal decline. From AD 244 there were fifty-five emperors in forty years, inflation began to spiral out of control, and civil wars sparked up as various generals vied for the top job, often splitting the empire. Pirate attacks became more frequent on the island, and disturbingly coordinated by barbarians who obviously sensed weakness; in 367 the Irish and Saxons attacked simultaneously from east and west, arguably the first instance of Anglo-Irish cooperation. Ireland's High King, Niall of the Nine Hostages, carried out a far bigger raid on Britain forty years later.[17]

Archaeological evidence also points to a grim picture. King's Weston in Bristol was destroyed in 367, but its last remaining inhabitant probably ended his days some time after that. The man, five feet tall and his fifties, had the side of his head lopped off by a sword, a cause of death that would not baffle any forensics expert.

Another surviving corpse from a villa suggests a life that had its ups and downs. On the one hand the man had delicately manicured fingernails, indicating a degree of civility; on the other he had been clubbed to death, garrotted, and then had his throat cut, so this was clearly a society with some problems. In 378 the Romans suffered their first major defeat at Adrianopole, at the hands of the Goths. It was the beginning of the end: from that year coins start to become rare, and by 430 they had been abandoned altogether in favour of bartering. Pottery production had stopped in 410, and what later became called the Dark Ages had effectively begun.

CHAPTER THREE

Angles, Saxons, and Jutes

Many of the characters involved in the Anglo-Saxon invasion are basically mythical but supposedly the Saxon warlord Elle arrived in what became Sussex around AD 470, followed by Cerdic in Wessex thirty years later, both of whom pushed the Britons out. According to the *Chronicle* Elle defeated the native tribe, Hesta's Folk, whose name survived in Hastings, while another Saxon leader called Port arrived in 501 and with "his two sons Bieda and Mægla came to Britain with 2 ships to the place which is called Portsmouth and slew a young British man, a very noble man,"[18] but this may be a very convoluted explanation for how the city got its name—rather than just the obvious "mouth of a port."

In 577 the Saxons completed their conquest by capturing the Severn Estuary, and so cutting the native territory in two. The Britons now held on to Wales, West Wales (as the south west of England was called), and Cumbria, the name of which is related to the Welsh Cymru, and which was not conquered by the Angles until much later.

This situation was mirrored all over western Europe. Elsewhere the Saxons also moved into central Germany, in what is now Saxony, while the Frisians occupied a region on the modern day Dutch/German border. The Franks overran the north of Roman Gaul, where they adopted the local Latin dialect that would become French. The Vandals in Spain and the Lombards in Italy also eventually became Romanized, largely because those provinces had stronger Roman institutions, but in contrast the Anglo-Saxons did not become in any way Romanized. It's possible this is because the Britons in the southern lowlands had spoken Latin, while British was spoken in the north, and that neither language was therefore strong enough to resist Old English.

There's a fierce debate in academia about how many Anglo-Saxons actually arrived, and whether they drove most of the natives out or whether a small number intermarried with the locals ("marry" perhaps being a bit of a euphemism—it wasn't a great age of romance). Some think the Anglo-Saxons were small in number, perhaps as few as one in twenty of the overall population, while other studies suggest that about one-third of English DNA is Anglo-Saxon in origin, and far higher in the east of England.[19] One study of male chromosomes showed that Englishmen even from the west of the country were more closely related to the Norwegians than the Welsh less than 100 miles away, and there hasn't been a Viking raiding party in over a millennium. However, to make matters more confusing, there is also the theory that the Angles and Saxons might have always lived in Britain, at least before the Romans, and that during the imperial period the east of the country was already German speaking (maybe Boudicca had blonde hair). DNA research certainly shows that people have been crossing the North Sea for thousands of years, so it's not impossible.

Certainly, most natives would have stayed behind after the Saxon conquest until their descendants eventually adopted Old English; a seventh-century law of King Ine of Wessex describes how the Britons are permitted to live in peace in their villages, as long as they keep themselves to themselves, and at least one archaeological find has turned up by a river a Saxon settlement coexisting with a British one on the other side. There were still British speakers in East Anglia as late as 700, while Britons still had their own district in Exeter until the tenth century, in an area known as Britayne—Little Britain—until much later.

The British resistance to the invasion was recalled in epic poems which chart romantic and dashing but highly unsuccessful military adventures. Aneirin, living in what is now Cumbria, wrote the poem *Y Gododdin* in the seventh century recording the British-Saxon wars. In particular it remembers the dead of a British tribe called the Gododdin who attacked the Angles in what is now North Yorkshire around AD 600; the Britons were led by the unpronounceable Mynyddog Mwynfawr, who managed to get every one of his soldiers killed in this not very successful enterprise.

The wars lasted about a century in total. Around the year 700 a British monk by the name of Nennius first wrote about the exploits of a leader who roused the Britons from defeat and won twelve battles, only to end in glorious failure with inevitable defeat, and death, sometime between 515 and 537, at the Battle of Camlann. It grew to become the most famous legend in the world, the story of a man who, despite his exploits being recorded only hundreds of years later and by some of the biggest liars in history, still inspires hopeful treasure hunters to traipse around the West Country looking for his castle. His name, of course, was Arthur, and legend has it that the king of Britons did not die and is only sleeping, ready to reawaken at Britain's hour of need. So, is there any truth in the story?

No.

Of all the tales about Arthur—the sword in the stone, the round table, Camelot, the lady of the lake, and Merlin—probably the only bit of truth is that someone called Arthur, or more likely Artorious or Ambrosius Aurelianus[20], had one or two battles with the Saxons. Most of the legend comes from Geoffrey of Monmouth, an imaginative historian living in the twelfth century. Geoffrey wasn't too interested in tedious historical procedures like using primary sources, written evidence, or archaeological finds, and preferred to just take a good story and throw in a few busty maidens, mad wizards, and fairies to liven things up. He also confidently stated that the Welsh arrived in Britain from the ancient city of Troy (in modern Turkey) after its destruction by the Greeks, and that Britain was previously inhabited by a race of giants, so we can't be entirely sure he was accurate about everything. Backing up his story, Geoffrey said he had learned all about Arthur from "a certain very ancient book" he found in Oxford, without ever revealing it. But he told great stories, and these were tremendously popular all over the continent. Later the Arthur story was cynically embellished by Richard the Lionheart, who just before setting off on a very costly crusade miraculously discovered the bodies of Arthur and his wife Guinevere at Glastonbury Abbey, as well as Arthur's sword.

This was a period of very scarce knowledge, after all. For example the *Annals of Wales*, the only record of that country at the time, gives as its only news for the whole year 447: "day dark as night," which doesn't give us much to work on.[21] *The Annals*, which may date to the tenth century but probably later, mention twelve of Arthur's battles in total, all of which have a religious air: "The eighth battle was in Fort Guinnion in which Arthur carried the image of St Mary, forever virgin, on his shoulders and that day the pagans were turned to flight and a great slaughter was made on them through the virtue of our Lord Jesus Christ and through the virtue his mother St Mary the Virgin." The twelfth battle was at Badon Hill, where according to the Welsh historian Nennius he allegedly killed 960 of the enemy singlehandedly, a spectacular achievement when one considers that he was also carrying a life-size replica of the "cross of our lord Jesus Christ" throughout the engagement in what can be only be described as an unorthodox strategy. The poem also says that no one else killed anyone in the entire battle, it was all Arthur; the Saxons just came at him, one by one, like villains in Jackie Chan films.

The legend survived in the remote, mountainous regions of Britain where the old language was still spoken, and in 1113 some

French visitors to Cornwall were told about King Arthur, laughed, and were pelted with vegetables. By the thirteenth century it had developed so that the Biblical character Joseph of Arimathea features as a character, having travelled all the way to Britain, something which would have been rather out of the way for a first-century Judean. (The name Camelot was made up by a French poet in the twelfth century.)

Today the location of a real "Camelot"—an Arthurian holdout against the Saxon invaders—remains a mystery; although Cornwall or Cadbury Hill in Somerset are possible candidates, there are dozens all over Wales and the northwest, and the Scottish borders are also a possibility. Wherever it is, it certainly wouldn't have looked like the magnificent medieval castle of Arthurian legend, which is based on the period, the fifteenth century, when the story was at its most popular. The real Camelot was probably no more than a couple of horse-drawn caravans and a ditch for urinating in, and had she existed Guinevere would have resembled a toothless Dark Ages hag dressed in old rags, rather than a beautiful medieval princess with a cone-shaped hat and perfectly shampooed Rapunzel-like flowing hair.

However, the Saxon kings identified as Arthur's enemies, King Cerdic and his son Cynric, are historical, or at least semi-historical, and went onto found the House of Wessex, from which the current royal family are descended.

The Warrior Ethic

Although some historians don't like the term, the period following Roman collapsed is known as the Dark Ages, because of the lack of evidence available. The first piece of written English dates from 450, and was scratched on stone using the ancient runic alphabet: "This she-wolf is a reward to my kinsman." But almost nothing would be written by any of them for another two centuries.

The Anglo-Saxons had eight words for spear, twelve for battle, and thirty-six for hero, but before the Romans introduced them they had no concept of table, pillow, or street. The oldest words in the English language, dating from this period, include "tits" and "fart," which suggest a society that must have had its moments, but was hardly on the verge of the renaissance. The language also had no future tense, which points to a certain lack of ambition.

The newcomers grew oats, rye, and barley, although especially the latter, which they called *bere*, and consumed in large quantities. They ate white bread, vegetables, and honey, and kept cattle, sheep, and pigs, but they were especially fond of horses, as the various chalk drawings illustrate.

The Anglo-Saxon calendar reflected how closely tied they were to the land. February was *Solmonath*, the month of dirt, "which in that month the English offered cakes" to their gods. April was *Eosturmonath*, "Easter month," after the goddess of spring who they made possibly quite cruel offerings to; October was *Winterfileth*, or "winter full moon"; after that came *Blotmonath*, or "blood month," when the cattle was slaughtered.[22]

There were a limited number of positions open to members of their society, to put it mildly; one was either a warrior, farmer, or slave, and between 10 and 25 percent of people were unfree, depending on the region (with more in poorer parts of the west). The slaves were probably mostly native Britons, who would have eventually been integrated into Anglo-Saxon society, although not in a very romantic, American Dream-like way.

Old English even had a word, *cyrelif*, for someone who had entered slavery by choice, because they were so indebted and life was too awful.[23] Above the slaves were the *coerls*, free peasants, although life probably wasn't that much fun for them, either (the word "churlish," as in sullen and ungrateful, comes from it). There must been class distinctions very early on, as the monk Bede recalls that after a battle in 678 an aristocrat called Imma was captured, and since the aristocratic prisoners were killed or enslaved, pretended to be a mere peasant (although we don't how he carried out this small talk) but was caught out 'by his face, dress and speech'; he was sold into slavery.

Life for everyone was pretty grim. At Buckland Cemetery in Kent, corpses from 480 to 750 suggest that while 20 percent of people died before eighteen, only 6 percent reached sixty, and "the lucky survivors commonly had dental problems, disabling damage to the joints, badly healed fractures and endemic diseases such as tuberculosis."[24] Childbirth was terrifyingly dangerous and although upper-class women were slightly less likely to die as a result, upper class men were more likely to die violently.

Although "Dark Ages" refers to the era's literary output, it was also a period of actual darkness; on top of everything else a huge volcano in AD 536 led to ten years without summer, and widespread hunger across Europe; the continent was also devastated by what became known as the Justinian Plague, after the Byzantine emperor of the time. All in all, it wasn't the best time ever to be alive.

The Anglo-Saxon social hierarchy was based, as with all societies at the time, on loyalty and reward. A man's obligation was to his lord, a word which derives from *loafward*, literally loaf giver, and this was usually the owner of the land he worked on. Under the Germanic concept of kinship, an individual held allegiance to the head of their kin group, at every level: child to father, father to extended family, and to local nobleman. The mutual obligations of giving service and receiving protection and financial support were the bonds that held society together.

In return for service the lord was expected to provide his men with wealth. The Anglo-Saxon poem *The Wanderer*, written around the tenth century but believed to have been composed as early as the seventh, features an exile speaking to his former lord as "gold friend" sitting on a "gift-throne." In the epic *Beowulf* Hrothgar's wife reminds him at one point: "Accept this cup, my loved lord, treasure-giver; O gold-friend of men."

Tiw-day, Woden-day, Thor-day, Frigg-day

Alfred the Great's Christianity was central to his life, his identity, the reforms he made, and his struggle against the heathen Vikings. Although the Danes were a different people, it was mainly their religion that separated them from the English; some Saxons went pagan under Danish rule and so in effect became Danes, while Vikings who converted stopped being Vikings. This is why Christian rulers were always trying to get them to accept baptism, even when the Danes were obviously only pretending to convert. Yet Alfred's kingdom had only been Christian for two centuries, and owed its conversion to a couple of Italians.

The early Anglo-Saxons believed they'd go to Valhalla when they died,[25] an afterlife that appears considerably more violent than the Christian heaven, with even children buried with their swords to bring with them. Valhalla also featured other activities, though: a grave found at Prittlewell, near Southend, included a sword, shield, spear, camping stool, two drinking vessels, a lyre, and some dice.

They worshipped the Norse gods, among them the goddess of war, Freyja, who rode a chariot pulled by two cats; her brother Frey the god of peace; and four others whose legacy lasted longer, Tiw, Woden, Thor, and Frige, giving us the days Tuesday–Friday (Saturday kept its Latin name).[26]

Norse paganism probably had a very dark side. The eighth-century monk Bede suggested that in the old days there may have been human sacrifices to Eostre, the Norse goddess of dawn and fertility, so called because the sun rises in the east. Whether Eostre was even a bona fide Norse deity is a matter of contention, as we only have Bede's word to rely on, but the name survives in Easter, spring being the time of year when human sacrifices would have taken place in most parts of the world to appease whatever cruel and petty god was in charge of crops.

At the other end of the Valhalla pecking order was Weland the Smith, Norse god of ironwork who, like his Greek equivalent

Vulcan, was disabled—the only difference being that Weland was deliberately crippled by a king to make him stay in his service. He then murdered the man's son and raped his daughter. If men make their gods in their own image, it certainly doesn't say much for Anglo-Saxon employment practices.

As they spent their days fighting and drinking, the Norse gods can't have known their days would be soon be over, at the hands of an urbane, sophisticated, bookworm Jewish God with an overbearing mother. By the late sixth century Rome, once a city of one million people, had shrunk to a desolate town of a few thousand, in constant fear of invasion and no longer even enjoying basic plumbing. It did, however, have two institutions still functioning: the Catholic Church, and a slave market. Under Pope Gregory I the Church had effectively taken over what was left out of the town, establishing it as the headquarters of western Christianity (Constantinople also claimed leadership of the Christian world and eventually the two would split in the Great Schism). Gregory was a great reformer who lifted the Church out of the dark ages, although he could be a touch authoritarian; a monk from his monastery once confessed to stealing some coins, so Gregory ordered for him to die alone and his corpse thrown on the rubbish pile, as penance for his sins.

One day during the 570s, several years before he became pontiff, Gregory was walking around the marketplace when he spotted a pair of blond-haired pagan slave boys for sale. Thinking it tragic that such innocent-looking children should be ignorant of the Lord, he asked a trader where they came from, and was told they were "Anglii," Angles. Gregory, who was fond of a pun, replied, "not Angles, but angels," a bit of wordplay that still works fourteen centuries later. Not content with this, he asked what region they came from and was told "Deira" (today's Yorkshire). "No," he said, warming to the theme and presumably laughing to himself, *de ira*—they are blessed. Impressed with his own punning, Gregory decided that the Angles and Saxons should be shown the true way. (A further embellishment has the Pope punning on the name of the Deiran king, Elle, by saying he'd sing "ha*ll*eluiah" if they were converted, but it seems dubious: How many puns about Dark Ages England can someone make in a row?) The Anglo-Saxons were very fond of wordplay, which feature a great deal in their surviving literature; again, without spoiling the story, we probably need to be slightly skeptical about whether Gregory actually said any of this.

The Pope ordered a Sicilian abbot called Augustine to go to Kent to convert the heathens. Having enjoyed a nice life in Rome, we can only imagine how Augustine must have felt about his new posting to a cold, faraway island populated by savages and skinheads, and he initially gave up halfway through his trip, leaving his entourage in southern Gaul while he went back to Rome to beg Gregory to call the thing off. At this point Augustine apparently had a dream in which St. Peter told him something to the effect that if he didn't continue he wouldn't have any need for warm clothes in the afterlife.

Post-apocalypse Britain must have seemed like an unimaginably grim posting for the priest. Still, in the misery-ridden squalor and obscurity that was sixth-century Britain, Kent was the closest thing to a happening place. It was near to Gaul, which had been overrun by the Franks in the fifth century but which had basically maintained Roman institutions and culture; the Frankish king Clovis had converted to Catholicism a century before after relentless pressure from his wife, and then as now people in Britain tended to ape the fashions of those across the water.

The barbarians of Britain were grouped into tribes led by chieftains, the word for their warlords, *cyning*, eventually evolving into its modern usage of "king." There were initially at least twelve small kingdoms, and various smaller tribal groupings, although by Augustine's time a series of hostile takeovers had reduced this to eight—Kent, Sussex, Essex and Wessex (the West Country and Thames Valley), East Anglia, Mercia (the Midlands), Bernicia (the far north), and Deira (Yorkshire). Of the other, earlier mini-kingdoms, such as Lindsay (today's Lincolnshire) and Hwicce (Gloucestershire/ Worcestershire), we know very little except a confusing list of kings with names like Ethelweard and Ethelherd. When Bernicia and Deira merged into Northumbria the system became known as the Heptarchy, literally the seven realms, one of many aspects of medieval English history that inspired *Game of Thrones*, along with the ceaseless violence.

In 597, when Augustine finally finished his long trip, Kent was ruled by King Ethelbert, great-grandson of Hengest, sometimes referred to as *bretwalda*, a term invented a bit later which translates as "wide ruler," although it came to mean "ruler of Britain," and denoted the strongest ruler on the island.

The king of Kent was married to a strong-willed Frankish princess called Bertha, and luckily for Augustine, Bertha was a Christian. She had only agreed to marry Ethelbert on condition that she was allowed to practice her religion, and such was her piety that she kept her own personal bishop.

Bertha persuaded her husband to talk to the missionary, and it's a sign of how suspicious the pagans must have been that at first the king made Augustine stay on the Isle of Thanet, now a slightly run-down region of ex-seaside resorts but which was then an island cut off by a channel. The king was acutely paranoid that the Italian would try to bamboozle him with witchcraft; even when Ethelbert agreed to meet him it had to be under an oak tree, which to the early English had magical properties that could overpower the foreigner's sorcery. (Oak trees had a strong association with mysticism throughout Europe, being seen as the king of the trees and associated with Woden, Zeus, Jupiter, and all the other alpha male gods.)

After being persuaded by his wife, Ethelbert allowed Augustine to baptize 10,000 Kentishmen, according to the histories. (This is probably a wild exaggeration; 10,000 is often used as a figure in medieval history, and usually just means "quite a lot of people." It could have been four guys and a dog for all we know.)

Although Ethelbert stood firm in his refusal to convert himself, he let the Christians settle in his capital Canterbury, which so became the headquarters of the English church. Ethelbert told Augustine: "Your words and promises are fair indeed, but they are new and strange to us, and I cannot accept them and abandon the age-old beliefs of the whole English nation." That wasn't enough for Bertha, and eventually, in 597, Ethelbert agreed to be baptized, and later that year Augustine became the first primate of England (the title would later be Archbishop of Canterbury).

Various other Christian missionaries would follow St. Augustine over to Britain, from southern Europe, North Africa, and the Middle East, going up and down the island teaching the faith, as well as Latin, Greek, art, and literature. For with Christianity came other aspects of Roman civilization; Ethelbert issued the oldest English coins and was the first Anglo-Saxon king to introduce law codes, a central part of King Alfred's idea of kingship which he was to imitate. Ethelbert's legal code was probably influenced by the Franks, and his in-laws, who had also introduced something similar around the time. The Laws of Ethelbert were not only the first works of written English, but also the first laws written in any native European tongue since the fall of Rome, and the first in any Germanic language.

The very first act of written English law deals with theft from church property, and that was probably because churchmen generally wrote the laws, since they were the only people who could read. It's a sign of how powerful the Church became that under the Laws of Ethelbert's great-great-grandson Wihtred (who ruled from 690 to 725) a bishop's servant receives the same protection as a king's servant, the Church is free from taxation, while there are also fines for "sacrificing to devils." Wihtred's laws also set a fine for priests too drunk to say Mass, which suggests this may have not been an entirely uncommon situation.

Curiously, considering the feminist movement at the time was in its infancy, Ethelbert was very progressive in passing a law allowing women to leave their husbands if there was just cause.

But Augustine's work fell to pieces when Ethelbert died and his half-witted son Eadbald took over and reverted to the old pagan ways, even marrying his stepmother (family values which the Christians disapproved of, although it made financial sense by keeping the inheritance together). Two of the three bishops in England, Mellitus of London and Justus of Rochester, ran off to France, but the other, Lawrence, stood his ground. Luckily Lawrence persuaded the new king to come back on board, convincing him that St. Peter had physically attacked him because the king had forsaken God. Eadbald, afraid for his friend's safety, dumped his wife/step-mother, had had in the meantime gone insane, as a monk recorded with some glee.

Augustine didn't do so well with the native Britons. When they arrived to meet him a few years later, he didn't get up from his chair, and they took this for arrogance;[27] as a result there developed a huge dispute between the Celtic and English churches which was sort of resolved when the King of Northumbria, Ethelfrith the Ferocious, killed a load of monks.

Ethelbert's sister had married the king of Essex, the weakest of the seven kingdoms, and their son allowed the Christians to settle in his capital, Lundenwic, where they built a church in honor of St. Paul. Ethelbert's daughter Ethelberga, meanwhile, married Edwin, king of Northumbria, who had in the meantime taken an interest in the religion, and would spread it across England.

CHAPTER FOUR

The Heroic and Utterly Ghastly World of Beowulf

In 1939 archaeologists made one of the greatest discoveries in British history at a spot called Sutton Hoo in Suffolk. It had long been rumored that the area, which featured lots of old, clearly man-made mounds, had some association with ancient kings. John Dee, who was Elizabeth I's advisor-cum-witch in residence during the sixteenth century, had tried digging around the spot; a century later, in 1690, a crown had been found but, annoyingly for historians, melted down. But what they found on August 23 that year was a glimpse into what is sometimes called the heroic age. In it was a longboat, in the center of which was a wooden chamber with a helmet and sword, some spears, a battle axe, a shield decorated with bird and dragons, drinking horns in silver, a silver bowl from Byzantium, ten shallow silver bowls, some more bowls, spoons, a gold buckle, a huge purse, nineteen pieces of jewelry, and forty coins from France.[28] It was one of the most amazing discoveries in history but, unfortunately, people were for some reason rather distracted in August 1939 and maybe didn't want to be reminded about a previous, highly successful German invasion of Britain.

Sutton Hoo dates from the seventh century, a time when Suffolk was part of the kingdom of East Anglia, and the burial site contains both pagan and Christian objects, which suggests that the kings were hedging their bets. Despite being a burial site, there's no actual body, although they later found an empty coffin, and it's probable that an East Anglian king was laid to rest here, although which one we don't know for sure.

The best known monarch of the time was Redwald, from a dynasty called the Wuffingas, after their founder, Wuffa, who may have come from Sweden originally, and the famous helmet found at Sutton Hoo (in fact just a few fragments) has come to be associated with him. After Ethelred of Kent, Redwald of East Anglia was the next king to be recognized as *bretwalda*; he was regarded as a great king, as he won some important battles, but not much else is known of him.

Despite this exciting find, it was in Northumbria, the most northerly of the kingdoms, where Anglo-Saxon culture first began to flourish. Northumbria—the Humber river traditionally marks the start of the north of England—arose out of two smaller kingdoms, Deira and Bernicia, a union that came about through the joining of two not very happy families. King Ethelfrith of Bernicia, known as the Ferocious perhaps because he wiped out a party of monks who'd turned up for peace negotiations, which turned out to be very brief, had united the two realms after he married the queen of Deira and killed her father; he also attempted to kill her brother Edwin, who fled first to Wales and then to East Anglia. Apart from that the marriage seemed to be happy.

As well as fighting family members, Ethelfrith was also locked in constant wars with the various Anglo-Saxon, British, and Gaelic-speaking peoples to the west and north. Before Alfred laid down the rudimentary workings of a state, the Dark Ages economy relied mainly on cattle rustling and capturing metal from opponents in battle; there was no way of building up the state through any sort of economy, so the measure of a king's worth was how much he could beat his neighbors in futile wars, until eventually he was killed by someone else (the main difference Christianity brought at first was that the Church got one-third of the booty). Of six East Anglian kings living around the time of Sutton Hoo, five died violently and the other's fate remains a mystery. One pagan king, Penda of Mercia, killed three Anglian kings in a row, while the fourth sided with him, only to die fighting.

Ethelfrith convinced Redwald to kill Edwin, but during his darkest hours a stranger came to the Northumbrian exile warning him to flee, and by later accounts this savior was revealed to be Paulinus of York, another Italian churchman who must have been wondering what on earth he'd done to end up in this place. Paulinus had been brought over by Edwin's Kentish Christian wife Ethelberga, who now found herself an exile in East Anglia.

Instead of killing Edwin, however, Redwald had been persuaded by his wife (an adamant pagan) to spare his life, and so instead the two men marched north and killed Ethelfrith, with Edwin taking the throne.

Edwin was unsure about signing up to this strange new religion, and so held a council to debate the matter, the main focus being whether the old gods had favoured them in battle. The man-god relationship in pagan times was openly superficial, with men worshipping deities on account of what they brought to the relationship, and dumping them if they were thought responsible for military defeat or a poor harvest, or if they just found a more fashionable god. After the leaders had debated the matter for a while, a humble counselor popped up with these words:

"The present life of man, O King, seems to me, like the swift flight of a sparrow through the room wherein you sit at supper in winter, with your companions, and a good fire in the midst, while the storms of rain and snow prevail outside. The sparrow, I say, flying in at one door and immediately out at another, whilst he is within is safe from the wintry storm; but after a short space of fair weather, he immediately vanishes out of your sight into the dark winter from whence he had emerged. So this life of man appears for a short space, but of what went before, or what is to follow, we know nothing. Therefore, if this new teaching has brought any more certain knowledge, it seems only right that we should follow it."

It remains one of the most moving passages from Old English, and is certainly more impressive than Ethelbert's reason for converting, which seems to have been simply to please his wife and have an easier life.

The first thing the new Christians did was smash up all the old pagan shrines. In fact the high priest Coifi asked if he could lead a twenty-mile procession to the pagan temple and desecrate it by throwing a spear into the gods' sanctuary, which he did, much to the bafflement of onlookers who wondered if he had lost his marbles. Coifi's rather childish gripe was that he wasn't paid as much as his contemporaries, which he blamed not on the king but on the gods, proving there are few things more dangerous than an embittered employee, even for an immortal.

Edwin went on to rule a largely peaceful kingdom, even if it inevitably ended with his violent death, in a battle with the Mercians. It was such a golden age that, according to the monk Bede, "in the days of Edwin a woman with a baby at her breast might have travelled over the island without suffering an insult" (he may have been a bit rose-tinted about that—crime rates at the time would have been absurdly high, and anyone travelling in groups of less than thirty could expect something terrible to happen to them). It was also noted that Edwin built drinking fountains across the highways of his realm, so that travellers could have water during their relaxing journey through the kingdom.

Traces of Edwin's hall in Yeavering were discovered in the mid-twentieth century; the site consisted of around ten buildings, including one, labelled "DI," which the archaeologist described as being an example of "strange incompetence" and designed to be rectangular but ending up as a rhomboid; after it fell down, another was built in its place, which also had wonky walls. After the Romans, pagan Anglo-Saxon England must have seemed quite desolate.[29]

The Northumbrian kings had two seats, the other being Bamburgh, on the coast; Bamburgh castle was eventually destroyed by the Vikings and rebuilt by the Normans, before being restored by eccentric Victorian industrialist William Armstrong, who had made his money by inventing the hydraulic crane and modern artillery.[30]

Kings rarely got much time to do anything before being fatally wounded. After Redwald's death his son Eorpwald embraced Christianity fully, and for his troubles was murdered by his subjects in 627. Four years later his half-brother Sigibert took the throne and became a Christian himself, but was then killed in 637 by his cousin Anna (a man). King Penda of Mercia then killed Anna and gave the kingdom to Anna's brother Ethelhere; Ethelhere and Penda were then killed in 654 at the battle of Winwed near Leeds, the first great battle of note in Saxon England; this involved the armies of four different kingdoms and a frightening number of odd-sounding barbarians slaughtering each other. Though records of this period are shaky, the scribes record that only two princes on the losing side escaped that day, including Cadfael "battle-dodger," one of the less impressively nicknamed early kings. His escape is self-explanatory.

All the Anglo-Saxon kingdoms were dominated by the never-ending violent struggles between various warlords; battles were frequent, and just as likely to involve two factions from within a kingdom. Far from being great Cecil B. DeMille events, most of these fights usually involved only about fifty or sixty men on each side, although Penda of Mercia's may have been several thousand strong. *Here* was the name given to an army (related to *Wehr* in German, as in *Wehrmacht*), and by the laws of King Ine a *here* was considered anything over thirty-five men, so the battles of the age were very small affairs, rather like fights outside pubs in English town centers.

To get some impression of what these scenes would have looked like it's worth knowing that during this pagan period people's faces were often painted or tattooed, men and women dyed their hair, with men going for blue, green, and orange locks, while everyone wore gold bracelets, as did the Vikings later.

After Edwin's death the different parts of Northumbria split once again, and Ethelfrith's son Eanfrith ruled Bernicia, the people reverting to the "abominations" of paganism in Bede's words, whatever that means. Paulinus fled, leaving another Italian, James the Deacon, all alone to run an isolated church in the wilds of Deira. Luckily Northumbrian kings never lasted long, and Eanfrith was no exception; he had made a truce with the local British chieftain Cadwallon but after falling out he went off with twelve soldiers to negotiate peace. It's not recorded what they talked about but by the end of the meeting Eanfrith was dead.

He was replaced by his brother Oswald, who once again united Deira and Bernicia after defeating Cadwallon. Since his uncle Edwin probably wanted him dead, Oswald had grown up in exile in the Gaelic-speaking world in what is now the west of Scotland, along with his younger brothers Osguid, Oswiu, Oslac, Oslaph, and Offa (Anglo-Saxons had the habit of giving their children names all starting with the same letter). There he had converted to Christianity, probably more sincerely than Edwin, and went one better than his uncle by becoming an actual saint. Oswald earned this by establishing the faith in his kingdom, asking his Irish contacts to lend him a bishop; the first one they sent was apparently too austere, so instead they dispatched St. Aidan (Oswald, who spoke Gaelic, acting as his interpreter). Aidan established churches all over Northumbria and probably did more even than Augustine in making England Christian.

In fact the Irish generally played a huge part, through monasteries. Monasticism had begun in Egypt in the fourth century with St. Anthony the Great, a holy man from Alexandria who fled to the desert to escape the attention of adoring intellectuals and other pseuds, his fans rather annoying him. Instead the city folk followed him to his hermit's cave, and then to the desert, and realizing he'd never escape from them he established a community of hermits. And so the first monastery, St. Anthony's, was created and by the fifth century there were 700 around the eastern Mediterranean. The idea really picked up in Ireland soon after the country was converted to Christianity by St Patrick in the fifth century. Irish monks in particular loved the austerity and self-inflected misery associated with the religious life, and the country's harsh environment provided the perfect backdrop; the most extreme was Skellig Michael, off the coast of Kerry, an isolated mountain island that is absurdly dangerous to climb up and can only be reached on calm days.[31] There was almost certainly some competition among Irish men to find the most inconvenient and uncomfortable place to settle down in, to show how holy they were.

In doing so Irish monks helped to preserve many of the ancient texts. They even had wars about monastic books, of all things; in one debacle, called the Battle of the Book, which took place in the kingdom of Cairbre Drom Cliabh in north-west Ireland between 555 and 561, two clans went to war after St. Columba had illegally copied a version of the Psalms belonging to St. Finnian, most likely the only war to even begin over copyright infrigment. The battle between the two groups led to "thousands" of deaths.[32]

The religion spread across all of England, and the Anglo-Saxons in turn converted the Germans back in Saxony Overseas, as they called what is now Germany,[33] until last pagan stronghold Sussex succumbed. The South Saxons only changed religion in exchange for the Isle of Wight, which Wulfhere of Mercia (658–675) gave them on condition that they convert.

Pope Gregory I had declared that pagans should be tolerated, but the Christian rulers inevitably began persecuting them as soon as possible; a surviving manifesto states "If any witch, or wizard, or false swearer, or worshipper of the dead, or any foul contaminated, manifest whore, be anywhere in the land, man shall drive them out." Archbishop Theodore of Canterbury's *Penitential*, which was written after he died in the 690s, gives us some idea of the strange things people got up to in the old pagan days, among the punishments described being "If any woman puts her daughter on the roof or into an oven to cure a fever, she shall do seven years' penance."[34] Theodore of Canterbury was a remarkable figure; born in Syria to a Greek family, he had gone to Rome in his late fifties, which was extraordinary in itself, but aged sixty-six, he was sent off to run the Anglo-Saxon church, without any knowledge of the barbarians' language. The position had become available after previous archbishop Wighard had travelled to Rome in 667 in order to be consecrated by the Pope, and almost immediately died of plague. Theodore was only given the job because everyone else refused it, and so they just nominated the Syrian guy.

Theodore had been taught a classical Greek education in Constantinople, and for someone raised in the antique culture of the Hellenic world, Britain must have seemed like something from Conan the Barbarian. But despite his lack of knowledge of the place, Theodore stayed for twenty-two years, totally reorganizing the English Church.[35]

The Christians also banned the traditional Saxon custom of worshipping stones, and forbid the use of nails or any other iron tools on Good Friday, in remembrance of Jesus. Paulinus ordered a youth to shoot down a crow from a trees to prove to "those who were still bound . . . to heathenism" not to idolize birds.

But rather than banning them outright, the Christians simply coopted most of the pagan traditions, so that the festival of Christ's death kept the name Eostre, and the new churches were built on old pagan sites; many religious grounds dating back to pre-Celtic times can boast a continual history of worship encompassing Stone Age,

Roman and Saxon paganism, Catholicism, Protestantism, and Irish theme pub.

Some rulers hedged their bets; Redwald, a man self-confident enough to claim descent from Caesar, didn't abandon paganism altogether because he was scared of his wife. Instead the king had two shrines built next to each other, one for Christ and one for the old gods. (I'm sure God would understand, not being jealous or anything.)

Some hangovers from pagan times still exist today: The "Boar's Head Carol," sung every year at Queen's College, Oxford by a procession carrying a boar's head, almost certainly dates back to an early Anglo-Saxon offering to Freyja.

The Christian religion introduced the Anglo-Saxons to a more sophisticated Mediterranean world, and exposed them to the Roman culture that their primitive forefathers had ignored. Latin words entered the language for the first time, and some people began to read. Previously the Saxons had used the runic alphabet, which was rather limited; for example it had nothing to signify the "g" sound, and there was no spaces between words, so reading anything longer than a short list of who killed whom is maddeningly difficult.

Oswald, who had gone by the rather exaggerated title "emperor of all Britain," died fighting the Mercians in 642, and power passed to his brother Oswiu, who struggled to keep together the various factions in the kingdom. Oswald, having fallen in battle with pagans, was soon hailed as a saint; before his burial, a beam of light was seen coming out of his grave, and his cult spread across northern Europe, his image being found on various old churches in England and Germany. His head was taken to Durham cathedral and his arm ended up in Peterborough for some reason; a second head of Oswald's turned up in Frisia, where it was reverently received apparently without skepticism,[36] while others were found in Luxemburg, Switzerland, and Germany. As none of his contemporaries mentioned him having five heads—which probably would have been the first thing a casual observer mentioned—we can be fairly sure they aren't all authentic.

Meanwhile his successor Oswiu was a keen convert who sent clergymen all over England and forced King Siegeberht of Essex to build St. Peter's at Bradwell-on-the-Sea in 653, the oldest surviving Anglo-Saxon building. Oswiu's great achievement was to establish Whitby Abbey, appointing his cousin Hilda as abbess. Hilda, as a thirteen-year-old, was among those baptized by King Edwin in 627, but when in 633 Penda of Mercia overran the kingdom she was taken by Paulinus and her relative Ethelburga to Kent; at thirty-three she returned to Northumbria to become a nun. Life in the monastery was austere to say the least, with everything held in common and most days spent reading the Bible. Hilda died at the age of sixty-six, having spent seven years suffering from a fever, but under her rule Whitby had become hugely important as a place of learning.

It was here that Oswiu held a famous synod that decided the most contentious issues dividing the church in Britain, among them the dating of Easter (still a source of never-ending dispute in Christianity) and what haircuts monks should have; some of the monks, such as those at Lindisfarne, stormed out of the conference and refused to accept the rulings.

Since there were no universities for another 400 years, most cerebral activity took place in monasteries, where men and women could learn the classics and the Bible. Not only could women run monasteries, but they were often coed, with different nuns' and monks' chambers, a system later killjoys abolished. During Hilda's time a shy monk at Whitby by the name of Caedmon wrote the first English poems, indeed the first English of any sort, explaining the myth of creation, turning words into poetry like a cow turns grass into dung, as one contemporary said (it was meant as a compliment). *Caedmon's Hymn* was penned sometime between 660 and 680, and features the lines "Then the Guardian of Mankind adorned this middle-earth below, the world for men, Everlasting Lord, Almighty

King." If this all sounds vaguely familiar, it is because J. R. R. Tolkien, who wrote *The Lord of the Rings* and *The Hobbit*, was an Anglo-Saxon scholar.

The most famous early work of Old English, however, is *Beowulf*, which dates to between 680 and 800 as a written work, although far older as an oral tale, and which is the best guide there is to the culture of the early English. It is set in Scandinavia, the old country as it was then, at around the time of the Anglo-Saxon invasion of Britain, and tells of a warrior from Sweden who travels to Denmark to kill a monster called Grendel, then kills its mother at the bottom of a lake, then returns home and kills a dragon. Then dies. Beowulf is a Geat, a tribe from southern Sweden, and goes to Denmark to help King Hrothgar of the Scyldings, whose great hall Heorot is occupied by Grendel these past twelve years. The hero is a Christian and the poem was written after the Angles had converted but it clearly dated to a period before Christianity, and a heroic time of warriors when men were driven by fate—*wyrd*—from which we get the modern English "weird." It's almost melancholy in lamenting the loss of a far more violent past, the good old days when men were men, before the Christians stopped people fighting monsters or putting their daughters on roofs. Beowulf may even be a metaphor for the end of human sacrifice.

Having killed the "loathsome creature," Beowulf's life ends in failure, with his country overrun anyway. The ultimate conclusion of the poem is that all the fame Beowulf won in life is meaningless.

Meanwhile Oswiu was succeeded by his brother Osred, most famous for going around the convents of his kingdom groping nuns. After that Oswiu's son, the hugely obscure Eadfrith (670–685), perhaps invented the silver penny, the world's oldest surviving currency; his reign, however, came to a speedy conclusion when he went to do battle with the Picts at Forfar. He wasn't the only one to meet a grisly end. During its golden age Northumbria had sixteen kings in 100 years, and only three died peacefully on the throne; two were exiled, five deposed, three killed in battle, and two murdered. The war between the two rival clans continued throughout and was only resolved in 867 when the Vikings adjudicated by killing both claimants.

Bede

Most of what we know of the Dark Ages, and it was hardly a period of rolling news, comes from the Venerable Bede, a monk from Northumbria who spent almost his entire life in a monastery and yet was, without question, the greatest historian of the age (he was also, it has to be said, pretty much the only one).

Born in 672 in Wearmouth, now part of the industrial city of Sunderland, Bede was orphaned as a child, and at the age of twelve was sent to the nearby monastery at Jarrow in County Durham. Things didn't get off to a good start—a year later, in 686, some local villagers arrived looking for parsley, optimistically hoping that this might cure them of the plague. They infected everyone in the monastery, and when the disease had left, only Bede and the elderly abbot were alive; however, not to be put off by this staffing shortage, they continued the chanting as a duo.

Life in the monastery would have been grueling, with most of the monks' time spent laboriously writing and copying ancient writings from dawn until dark, in conditions so cold that the quills would turn to ice and slip out of their hands, Dark Ages monasteries in Northumbria not being heated (obviously). Making and writing a book was tediously laborious at the time; calves' skins were used as parchment and it took 500 of the animals to make a Bible. And yet Bede managed to write sixty-eight books, on subjects including philosophy, astronomy, grammar, and mathematics. So quickly had Northumbria progressed since conversion that Bede had access to 200 books, mostly from Italy, and this was more than either Oxford or Cambridge had at the start of the Tudor period seven centuries later.[37]

Bede's great book *The Ecclesiastical History of the English Nation*, written in Latin sometime around 731, was not only the first history of the Anglo-Saxons, but the first reference to an English nation, rather than a collection of tribal fiefdoms.[38] Because Bede was an Angle, he called the people of the seven kingdoms the English, although it might just have been Saxony, and was called *Saxonia* in Latin for a while (as well as Celtic names for their neighbors deriving from the same tribe, Finns still refer to the Germans as "Saska").

Considering the circumstances, Bede expressed a mindlessly underserved sense of national confidence, referring to the English as "God's destined race;" although why God would put his destined race on a rain-swept island in the middle of nowhere is anyone's guess. He also suggested that God himself gave them the land, justifying this logic with the argument that the Britons had invoked the Almighty's ire by failing to convert the Anglo-Saxon newcomers—as if asking, "Have you ever thought about Jesus?" to some marauding barbarian maniac would have done much good.

As well as history, he also recorded news from all over the country, even from far-off Sussex, where the South Saxons were reported jumping off a cliff during a terrible famine—at Beachy Head, still the most popular suicide spot in the country.[39] Bede's work was copied and sent around the country, the first time that men from the different kingdoms read about the rest of the island, but it was Alfred who had it translated from Latin into English.

Bede's legacy stretched further still. Europeans at the time dated the years using twenty-eight different methods, the most popular being from the foundation of Rome (731 BC), or from the start of a monarch's reign, a difficult task when there were seven English kings at any one time and their life expectancy tended to be quite short. Pious Bede thought it was more appropriate to measure from Christ's birth, an idea that had first been put forward by a Greek called Dennis the Little; thanks to Bede the terms Before Christ and *Anno Domini* (year of our lord) were popularized and soon the system was used all across Christendom (unfortunately Dennis was six years out; Jesus was probably born in 6 BC, but Bede can hardly be blamed for that).

Not bad considering where he was, or that he was blind for most of his life, so blind that on one occasions two monks once tricked him into saying Mass to an empty church.

After a lifetime of work, on the evening of May 25, 735 Bede dictated the last chapter to a lad named Wilbert, who followed his instructions to write down his words. While dictating his words, Bede said: "It is well finished. Now raise my head in your hands." Then he died. He worked, literally to the last minute, and was buried in Durham Cathedral, where the Latin inscription "here lie the venerable bones of Bede" were mistranslated into "here lie the bones of the venerable Bede," giving him the slightly odd name he has been known by since.

Bede was the greatest holy man of the age, although not the only one. Among many others, the most significant was St. Boniface, born around 675 in Devon, who became the patron saint of Germany after converting many people in that pagan land; inevitably he was hacked to death by some angry heathens in the Low Countries. These things never ended well.

Bede lived during what was later called the Northumbrian Golden Age; not only was the kingdom the most advanced in the British isles, but it was one of the most exciting in western Europe. The showpiece of this culture was the Lindisfarne Gospels, a multi-coloured masterpiece made at a time when most books only used three colours, laboriously written and illustrated in the Irish style by a monk called Eadfrith, and completed around 715 (Eadfrith was apparently also the first man to use a lead pencil).[40] The Gospels remained at Durham Cathedral until Henry VIII's goons stole them in the sixteenth century and brought them to London, and today the book rests at the British Library next to St Pancras station.

CHAPTER FIVE

Offa's Dyke

Although Penda of Mercia was eventually, and inevitably, killed in battle, during the eighth century power shifted towards Mercia, which in today's geography is roughly the English midlands, and centered on Tamworth in Staffordshire. Mercia translates as boundary, and it was founded by the most ferocious settlers on the frontier with the British, originating in what is now Derbyshire and going on to absorb a number of smaller tribes with very obscure-sounding names. As a basic rule Mercia and Northumbria were always at war; after Penda was killed the Northumbrians installed his son Paeda as a puppet, but Paeda was soon murdered, possibly by his wife, and his brother Wulfhere was put on the throne. Wulfhere converted to Christianity and this seemed to pacify the place a little bit, or at any rate the existence of monasteries gave unpopular kings somewhere to go when it all got too difficult; his immediate successors, Ethelred and Coenred, both retired to religious houses.

In 748 King Ethelbald (716–757) was recognized as *rex Sutanglorum*, king of the southern English; Ethelbald was a famous letch, a violator of men's wives and also "the brides of Christ," and eventually his behaviour led his own bodyguard to stab him to death. That same year in Wessex King Sigeberht was deposed by the witan, the ruling council, for his "unjust acts" and then outlawed to the Weald of Kent where a swineherd stabbed him to death in a blood feud.

Ethelbald's second cousin Offa murdered Ethelbald's successor Beornred a few weeks later and took the throne, reigning for forty years and becoming the most powerful Dark Ages king and a model for Alfred. During his reign Offa conquered the smaller kingdom-ettes of Sussex and Kent, and through extending to the English Channel he seems to have been hugely influenced by the more civilized, advanced kingdom of the Franks.

The Franks had been the first of the western barbarians to adopt Catholic Christianity, after God had helped King Clovis during a particularly tricky battle against another German tribe, the Allemani in 496.[41] But in the late eighth century Charlemagne was the first of the barbarian kings to really bring western Europe out of the Dark Ages, doing much to encourage literature and the arts and, more importantly, killing lots of people who got in his way; however, after slaughtering 4,500 Saxon noblemen for refusing to convert, Charles the Great mellowed in his old age, abolishing the death penalty for paganism.

Charlemagne's father Pepin had made himself king after deposing the descendants of Clovis, and had himself crowned by bishops, the first time a coronation took on its modern, religious nature. Charlemagne went one further by having himself crowned emperor in 800, setting the way for the Kingdom of the Franks to become France (although the Frankish rulers continued to speak a form of German for another 200 years). He also made his court a center of learning, employing perhaps the greatest Anglo-Saxon scholar of the age, Alcuin of York. In total more than 300 of Alcuin's letters have survived; during this period he wrote many grovelling things about King Offa when he was alive and some rather less flattering things after he had died.

Offa and Charlemagne corresponded by letter and exchanged gifts, although the emperor's were noticeably better. In 796 the

Frankish ruler sent a missive, calling Offa his "dearest brother," "strong protector of your earthly country," and "defender of the holy faith." The only other surviving correspondence from the ruler of the Franks is a letter written later that year, in which Charlemagne complains about his Anglo-Saxon counterpart selling him poor-quality cloaks and blankets.[42] The two monarchs also agreed for Charlemagne's son to marry Offa's daughter, but when the Mercian insisted that his son marry one of the Frank's daughters as part of the bargain, Charlemagne shut all Frankish ports to him; a no, in other words.

His new links to Francia seemed to give Offa ideas. He began to mint coins at Canterbury with his face on them, in the Roman style, showing Offa "with elaborately dressed hair arranged in curls, cut to give hints of light and shade" while "on others he is diademed and draped like a Roman emperor, and is also shown wearing rich jewels."[43] Offa's wife Cynethryth was the only Anglo-Saxon queen to ever appear on a coin, although this probably reflects less his love of a good woman than a growing pretentiousness about copying the Roman emperors (which, if his subjects had known about some of the maniacs who ruled the empire, might have concerned them).

Fashion was influenced by France, then as now, and Offa was the first ruler to adopt fancy continental styles of dress, so much so that Alcuin complained of the king's love of fashionable Frankish clothes: "Some idiot thinks up a new-fangled idea and the next minute the whole country is trying to copy it."

Offa seems to have been quite argumentative and his reign was also marked by the first case of conflict between kings and archbishops. He made the Pope divide the country into two areas because he didn't like the Archbishop of Canterbury, which the Pope agreed to do; after Offa died the Pope reversed it.

His second greatest legacy (although it may have been Ine of Wessex) was to build the Schola Saxonum, or Saxon School, a hostel for pilgrims in Rome, in an area of the city that was named after the

English travellers who went there. However, he is best remembered for the ditch he built to stop the Welsh entering his kingdom; Offa's Dyke is still, give or take a few miles, the modern boundary between England and Wales, and the physical remains are in place, just about.

After Offa died Kent rebelled under a priest called Eadberht Praen, who ended up being blinded and having his hands removed. Before he died, however, Offa had bullied the witan into accepting his son Ecgfrith as his heir, having him anointed as king in 787, in the Frankish style. Again, he was clearly influenced by Charlemagne, who had his own sons sent to Rome to emphasize his links with the old empire.

This was the origin of the religious element of royal coronations that continues to the present-day royal family, and which had been adopted by all the barbarian kings hoping some Roman charisma would rub off; one of the great attractions of Christianity was that kings were able to draw on Roman culture and prestige.

Unfortunately Offa's son Ecgfrith died just a few weeks after his father's own passing and the line came to an end. Alcuin said it was the will of God but heavily hinting it was all Offa's fault: "For truly, as I think, that most noble young man has not died for his own sins; but the vengeance for the blood shed by the father had reached the son. For you know very well how much blood his father shed to secure the kingdom on his son. This was not a strengthening of his kingdom but its ruin."

Alcuin never said this when Offa was alive, obviously; in fact he had written to him calling him "the glory of Britain, the trumpet of the gospel, our sword and shield against the enemy."

By the end of his reign Offa effectively ruled all of England, and were his successors to have been as successful as he, the country's capital might have been somewhere in Staffordshire. But it was never to be, for as anyone who has ever moved up in the world knows, the worst nightmare imaginable is when uncouth, distant relations turn up and spoil things. And the Anglo-Saxons had the worst relatives imaginable—the Vikings.

CHAPTER SIX

What the Vikings Did for Us

Vikings have traditionally got a bad press, being viewed in the popular imagination as a sort of ancient biker gang who went a bit overboard. On the other hand, recent historians have liked to focus on their commercial and sailing skills; as well as being heavily armed on their travels, they sometimes carried goods such as cloth for trade, no doubt marketed with the same emphasis on intimidation used by unemployed teenagers selling mops to an old age pensioner.

As well as this, we should remember their nation-building in Russia and their achievement in reaching as far as North America. And they were certainly smart sailors: Raven Floki, known as Floki the Lucky, discovered Iceland by the clever trick of capturing three ravens and keeping them on board, then releasing them and following the birds, which can sense where the nearest land is.

Obviously none of this revisionist history would have appeared very reassuring to a Northumbrian monk who'd just had his monastery plundered and burned to the ground. Or to the poor souls who found their resting place at a Viking burial ground dating from 879, which contains two murdered slave girls beside a Viking warrior, as well as the jumbled remains of hundreds of men, women, and children, just so the Norseman could torment Saxons in Valhalla. Despite the modern fashion for painting Vikings as just rather aggressive salesmen, the Danes and Norwegians were a menace, rightly compared to a plague by anyone unfortunate enough to have any contact with them.

No one called them Vikings at the time; that word simply means raider[44] and only became common when the Icelandic sagas of the eleventh century were popularized in Victorian times. To the Saxons they were called Danes, even if they were often Norwegian; both nationalities tended to rape and pillage, so it didn't really make much difference which freezing hellhole they came from. More usually they were called "heathens" or *pagani* (pagan).

Neither did they wear horned helmets in battle, as they are traditionally depicted in cartoons, an idea that mainly came along because of Richard Wagner's slightly sinister nineteenth-century operas about the glories of the Nordic race in olden times. The Vikings wore the same conical helmets as everyone else, although they did occasionally place horns or other ornaments on burial sites; in fact most of the time they didn't wear any helmets.

The adventurous Greek mariner Pytheas may have visited Scandinavia in the fourth century BC; he wrote of a place called Thule where the people lived off wild berries because of a lack of crops and cattle. The Romans called the area *Scadinavia*, which may mean "dangerous island," because the sea was dangerous, rather than the people. An N was later added in.

Although early Norse history is a mixture of hearsay, myth, and obviously made-up stuff, the earliest Swedish dynasty to create some sort of state was most likely a group called "the Ynglings." Being a Viking king was a tough job; one early ruler, Domaldi, was offered up by his own people as a human sacrifice to the gods after the crops failed in a moment of pure *Wicker Man* horror. Another Yngling king, Donnar, died "racked in pain in Sweden" although no further details are given. Then there was the strangely named king Eystein Fart, who died when a warlock he robbed, Skyjold of Varna, made a gust of wind rock his ship and he drowned.[45]

The original center of ancient Scandinavian culture was most likely Old Uppsala, near modern-day Stockholm, and there archaeologists have discovered burial grounds of ancient kings, who were sent to Valhalla with horses, dogs and other animals, weaponry, grave-goods, and everyday objects as well as rare treasures. Later writers say there were human sacrifices at this spot, which took place every nine years when nine males of each species—including men— were killed to please the gods. One source says that at Uppsala the corpses of the victims were left on display even after Christianity had arrived in the region, and that Christians had to pay a tax to avoid getting involved in the colourful local festival, which they were presumably happy to. Even if this was later Christian propaganda, there is certainly forensic evidence of the practice; a hill at Ballateare on the Isle of Man contains what may be the only human sacrifice known from Vikings in the British Isles, a female with a hole in her head.

Ibn Fadlan, a tenth-century Arabic traveller who spent time with the Vikings in Russia, whom he affectionately called "Allah's filthiest creatures," recalled how one young woman was sacrificed to accompany her master into the afterlife, after first having sex with all the men in the group, presumably after been drugged. It's easy to see how prudish Christians might have disapproved of all these shenanigans.

Norse religion was certainly quite cruel; the head of the gods was Odin to the Scandinavians, Woden or Wotan to Germans further south, and he was especially worshipped by raiders. Odin was the god of battle and poetry, praised at banquets as a back-handed compliment to the host, and was known for his wisdom, but also his battle skills; riding on his eight-legged horse Sleipnir, Odin was also called the Charging Rider, the Spear Lord, the Army Father, the Battle Blind, and the Author of Victory, which says something about their culture (compare with Jesus's titles, among them Prince of Peace, Lamb of God, Good Shepherd, etc.).

Odin was also patron of the men who stood at the front of battle, who wore no armor and were said to take on animal characteristics as they went to into a frenzy; these warriors were known as wolf-skins and bear-shirts, *ulfhednar* and *berserkir*, from where we get the word "berserk." Although famed and feared, later sagas are less flattering to berserkers; one possible theory it that this is because earlier songs would have been sung with the minstrel in the same room as the berserker he was singing about, presumably glaring at him as he chose his words carefully.[46] There is also the theory that berserkers were largely propaganda stories designed to scare people and such frenzied behaviour would actually have been counterproductive, breaking up the lines; in Iceland acting like a berserker was banned during battle because it just got everyone killed.[47]

Bjorn (bear) and Ulf (wolf) were both common names among Norse men, although they're better remembered for their epithets, among them Erik the Victorious, Bodvar the Wise, Eyjolf the Lame, Eyvind the Plagiarist, Halli the Sarcastic, Ivar Horse-Cock, Harold Wartooth, Wolf the Unwashed, and Thorkell the Skull-splitter. Women had colorful names too, like Thorkatla Bosom and Hallgerd Long-Legs.[48]

Odin was also called the Chooser of the Slain, the *valkojosandi*, and his female assistants were called *valkyrjur*; there were fifty-two of these Valkyries, among them Bright Battle, Ale-Rune, Taunts, War, Chaos, Devastation, Cruelty, Sword-Time, Killer, Unstable, and Bossy. According to Viking folklore, Odin and the Valkryies lead wild hunts across the sky, seen as the *aurora borealis*, or northern lights.

In Norse myth Odin tried to avoid death at the battle of the end of the world by hanging upside down for nine days from Yggdrasil, a tree in deepest Scandinavia; for doing this he somehow received the forbidden knowledge of the runes which told him about the end of the world. Odin was portrayed sometimes as an old man ravaged by time, with a spear, a staff, and two ravens, the god usually one-eyed or occasionally blind. He is also called Jolnir, an elderly spirit of winter invited into people's homes during the mid-winter festival of Yul; a sort of precursor to the central European Santa Claus, although somewhat less child-friendly and certainly not the kind of person you'd want visiting your house at Christmas these days. In Viking sagas Odin, like the other gods, interacted with people on earth; one Norse leader, Harald Wartooth, was visited by the god, who promised him invulnerability in return for the souls of the enemies he killed with his sword. Or so he claimed.

While those who fell in battle spent eternity in Valhalla, where they fought in the day and drank at night (anyone killed in the daytime would be brought back to life in time to join in the feasting), weaklings, mummy's boys, and bed-wetters who died peacefully went to a very cold place called "Hel." All in all Norse paganism looks like what you get if you let teenage boys design a religion, focused on fighting, fornication, and alcohol, whereas Christianity seemed to them like it was thought up by their mothers. The Vikings celebrated Yul, the midwinter festival, which involved drinking lots of ale and collecting cattle blood to turn into pudding, and which survives in our word Yuletide; it sounded like it was probably a bit more fun than the more somber Christian midwinter festival, Christmas, although you were probably more likely to end up getting stabbed.

Scandinavia was a society rich in fable and legend and strange creatures, as you might imagine of somewhere with months of long nights and high alcohol consumption; there were *Alfar*, or elves, and their dark cousins, *dvergar*, dwarves (there is never any suggestion that they are little, at least until the Christian age). Bad dreams supposedly came from myths about malevolent creatures called *mares*, often associated with horses, from where we get nightmare. There were other beings such as *thyrs* (ogres) and trolls, too, while important places had guardian spirits, *landvoettir*. Viking shamans were often Finno-Urgic people, the Norsemens' neighbors who they considered a bit weird.

The Vikings did have some curious quirks though. Norse women could divorce their husbands and keep their own surnames after marriage, and if they were together twenty years were entitled to half their possessions; overall they had far more power than women in any other society of the time, or most later. Scandinavian men were also known to wear bracelets and wash and look after their hair, and Norse haircuts became fashionable in Northumbria. This is not to distract from the essential cruelty of their society, illustrated by the imaginative punishments meted out for wrongdoings. Men caught committing adultery with another man's wife could be trampled to death by a horse; those who killed their brothers were hanged by their heels next to a live wolf, while arsonists were burned at the stake.[49]

Whatever the faults of a violent and cruel society, no one can deny that they went on some extraordinary adventures. One group of sixty-two ships, setting out from the Loire river in central France, where they had encamped, raided as far away as Moorish Spain. They eventually sacked Morocco before one party headed back, arriving in Ireland where they were called the "blue men" by locals. Some Norsemen even managed to head all the way around Gibraltar and into the Mediterranean. In 859 two Viking leaders called Haesten and Bjorn Ironside planned on sacking Rome but Haesten, thinking he had reached the Eternal City, instead attacked the small town of Luna, 300 miles north; to be fair, to people who came from fishing villages ruled by people with names like Ivar Horse-cock, any Italian city would have looked pretty much like Rome.

Scandinavian society was based on three social classes—the *jarl*, *karl*, and *prael*, or slaves, the latter of whom were given deliberately stupid names like Clott or Stinking for the men and Fat-thighs or Dumpy for the ladies, just as if their life wasn't terrible enough. Having said that, being a slave in Scandinavia wasn't the worst thing in the world; you could be liberated if you were lucky, and the children of female slaves and free masters could also be free.[50]

But for free men there was a certain equality, in that they shared their booty equally; the Norsemen held assemblies where they'd vote by brandishing their knives—"one man, one knife," you could call it. Their sense of comradeship was very strong, so much so that they went in for cutting their wrists and making themselves blood brothers.

The Vikings and the Anglo-Saxons were closely related by ancestry and language, since the latter had themselves only left Denmark three hundred years previously. But while the Saxons had settled down and found God, the Vikings were aggressive, pagan, and suffering serious overcrowding at home—and as far as the Saxons were concerned these invaders in their eighty-foot longboats may as well have come straight from Hell; indeed they were seen as punishment from God.

The monastery at Lindisfarne had been founded by St. Aidan in 635 on the same spot where a church still stands, and as Christianity had become established it, like all monasteries, had amassed a fair amount of wealth, since they were not subject to tax and monks did not have to join the army; in fact Bede said that many monasteries were in effect a scam where little prayer or anything constructive was done. But the idea that anyone might actually attack a monastery was utterly shocking.

A chronicler called Simeon of Durham wrote of the events of 793: "The pagans from the northern regions came with a naval force to Britain like stinging hornets and spread on all sides like fearful wolves, robbed, tore and slaughtered not only beasts of burden, sheep and oxen, but even priests and deacons, and companies of monks and nuns. And they came to the church of Lindisfarne, laid everything waste with grievous plundering, trampled the holy places with polluted steps, dug up the altars and seized all the treasures of the holy church. They killed some of the brothers, took some away with them in fetters, many they drove out, naked and loaded with insults, some they drowned in the sea."

The *Chronicle* report that at the time of the raid there were immense whirlwinds and flashes of lightning, and fiery dragons seen flying in the air. The Anglo-Saxons loved this sort of end-of-the-world drama, and were fond of doomsday-like poetry about Armageddon. The tenth-century poem *Christ III* imagines the day when the stars are scattered, the moon falls from the sky and the sun dies, leaving the world lit only by a blood-stained cross. It's quite a gloomy story, all in all.

Lindisfarne was obviously not the first raid, for the previous year Offa had imposed duties on churches in Kent for construction and repair of bridges and fortifications, and for expeditions *contra paganos marinos*. By 804 abbesses and abbots were beginning to locate monasteries away from the coast, with one Abbess Selethryth of Lyminge looking around Canterbury for a new home for their monastery, behind its city walls and away from the sea.

Despite the attacks many applied to join monasteries, whose members were exempt from military service—this didn't matter to the raiders, for whom monasteries weren't exempt from plundering. The Vikings despised Christianity as a weak and feminine, and boring, religion. The first Christian missionary to the Norsemen seems to have been the Northumbrian St. Willibrord in 714, who visited King Ongenus of the Danes, a man described as "fiercer than any wild beast, and harder than stone." Willibrord spent forty years as a missionary but had no luck with the Danes.[51]

Many did, indeed, attribute the attacks to divine anger. Alcuin, writing to King Ethelred of Northumbria, blamed the Viking raids on vice, corruption, "fornicating, adultery and incest" by nuns, short beards, luxurious clothes and even foxhunting by the clergy. Alcuin quoted the Book of Jeremiah: "Then the Lord said unto me, Out of the north an evil shall break forth on all inhabitants of the land." Alcuin, sounding like he was enjoying it, announced that "Behold, judgment has begun."

However, despite a widespread view that they were agents of God's anger, the reason that these wild beasts began terrorizing their neighbors was largely economic: the very north of Europe is poor in natural resources and from around 600 AD the region began to experience huge population pressure—between the eighth and eleventh centuries 200,000 people left Scandinavia to settle elsewhere.[52] They didn't always make ideal immigrants, it's fair to say. On top of this the development of new technology in shipbuilding allowed the Scandinavians to cross the North Sea in the eighth century, inside the famous vessels known as longships.

The year 795 saw the first raid on Ireland, which was even easier to attack for the Norsemen because it was divided into not several but hundreds of mini- and micro-kingdoms. The Scottish islands, perfect for the supreme seamen of the age, were also a target, and the Orkneys were the most heavily settled by the Vikings. Even the Picts, the famously terrifying tattooed maniacs of Caledonia who inspired the Romans to build a huge great wall to keep them out, got a hard time from the Vikings; one excavation from Scotland revealed a charred building, smashed up sculptures, and slashed-to-pieces corpses. There were occasional occupational hazards, however, to being a Viking. Sigurd the Powerful, first Norse earl of Orkney from 874, was killed in 890 after he had decapitated Pictish rival Mael Brigte the Bucktoothed in battle. The tragicomic mishap happened afterwards when Sigurd was riding around with Mael's head on his saddle, and Sigurd's leg was scratched by the dead man's eponymously large tooth. Poor Sigurd died from the infection.

But the Vikings then went quiet for forty years in England, for a simple reason. A year after the Lindisfarne raid they were delayed by bad weather at Jarrow during another excursion, and when they appeared at the riverbank the local men cut them to pieces, and sent the tortured corpse of their leader back to Scandinavia, which seems to have got the message across.

However, in 831, sixty ships appeared on the River Boyne in eastern Ireland and another sixty on the Liffey, and that same year between twenty-five and thirty-five vessels landed at Carhampton in

Somerset, right in the heart of Wessex. Saxon levies, farmers drafted into fight, came from two counties but were beaten; the *Chronicle* records that the next serious raid was in 835 in Sheppey, Kent.

In 842 the Danes attacked London, burning down the bridge. Seven years later a huge fleet, 350 ships strong, arrived and sacked Canterbury, and this time the invaders weren't just raiding and pillaging; they established a permanent home on Thanet in 850, the first time they wintered in England. Thanet was a wealthy area and strategically important for trading with France, and it was also home to nunneries, which tended to have plenty of gold. The Vikings then camped on the Seine for the winter of 852–853, for whenever things got a bit tricky in Britain they just went off to Francia, and vice versa.

Francia was unfortunately at this point in the middle of a civil war between Charlemagne's grandsons, who were fighting over their inheritance, and were ineffective as Viking raids increased along the entire west coast, a fleet of 100 attacking Paris in 845. The raiders were also active in the Low Counties and Aquitaine, in the south-west of France, which was so desolate after years of war and violence that chroniclers reported packs of wolves, 300 strong, roaming the countryside, devouring anyone the Vikings hadn't got yet.

England at the time was thinly populated, with almost no urban areas, no standing armies, and with much of it marked by waterways and marshes, so it was easy for seaborne raiders to cause havoc. Viking longboats were typically about the length of a tennis court, and carried between thirty and sixty men, so a group of thirty ships would have been terrifying; the Viking war-bands, called a *comitatus* by Latin-speaking chroniclers, consumed a ton of grain a day and so made hungry uninvited guests.

The Vikings did sometimes lose battles, such as in 860 when the West Saxons "fought against the enemy, and putting them to flight, made themselves masters of the field of battle," according to Asser, and the Norsemen "were cut down everywhere and, when they could resist no longer, they took to flight like women." However generally speaking the Vikings won, because their armies were composed of full-time warriors, while the Saxons were mostly farmers, even if major lords might have had their own small militias. In battle the Norse warriors used the bearded axe, the standard hooked axe one sees in medieval films, but also the Danish axe, which was larger and required two hands and was basically too unwieldy for all but the absurdly strong. The Saxons, meanwhile, were often only armed with whatever farmyard implements they could get their hands on.

A crisis turned into a national catastrophe in 865 with the arrival of the 3,000-strong Great Heathen Army, led by Halfdan, Ivarr, and Ubba, the three sons of the legendary Ragnar Lothbrok. Not much is known of these three men, except that Ivarr the Boneless may have had brittle bone disease, while Halfdan had the strange nickname "the Wide-embracer." Ragnar may have had another son, Bjorn Ironside, the legendary king of Sweden, if he existed.

Even less is definitely known about Ragnar, whose surname means "hairy trousers," acquired after he had worn special breeches to rescue his future wife from a monster, although he appeared in many folk stories. Ragnar's tales were manifold, and he "brought such carnage and died so often that he seems more like a figure in a Hollywood film than a man from real life."[53] In the *Tales of the Sons of Ragnar* the hero is killed by King Aelle of Northumbria after being thrown in a snake pit, but he suffered so many deaths it's hard to know which one could possibly be true.[54] *Ragnar's Saga,* as the Icelandic story is also called, says that he had only gone to England because he was jealous of his sons, and his untimely death there was apparently the cause of the invasion of England by the Danes, to avenge the death of a kinsman; although it's hardly like they needed a reason. No one is entirely sure if Ragnar existed, in fact; a Ragnar attacked Paris in 845, but we don't know if it's the same as Lothbrok. That Ragnar apparently ended up suffering a terrible death back in Denmark, his stomach bursting open as his guts spilled out, so this would make a subsequent invasion of England difficult.[55]

It happened that the Viking invasion took place during a period of great instability in the four English kingdoms; in this whole era just one Northumbrian king was peacefully succeeded by his son, while Mercia was being fought over by four different families, while also simultaneously at war with Wessex. The Great Army arrived en masse in East Anglia in 865, settling for the winter of 865-866, where according to the *Anglo-Saxon Chronicle* "they were provided with horses, and the East Anglians made peace with them." They then headed north and attacked the Northumbrian capital Eoforwic on November 1, 865, as the city was packed with people attending All Saints' Day Mass in its cathedral. This was a common tactic used by the Vikings, who knew that Christians would not be prepared on religious festivals. The two bickering Northumbrian kings Aelle and Osberht were both there, but were so busy arguing that they had not bothered to prepare for any attack, even though it was known the Vikings were nearby to the south. Aelle and Osberht both survived the assault, returning only once the Danes had left. However in a subsequent attack on the Norsemen Osberht was killed, while Aelle was put to death by Ivarr and Halfdan using an especially cruel form of execution called the blood eagle, supposedly in revenge for killing their father. The blood eagle involved the victim's ribs being ripped out and then removed while he was still alive (it probably took some skill), after which his lungs were removed and spread across his back; he was then beheaded and chopped up.[56] A puppet king called Egbert was installed, who after this display was understandably rather compliant; unable to pronounce the name Eoforwic, the Vikings called it Jorvik, from which we get York.

They then headed south, wintering in Nottingham in the English midlands in 867. At this point a combined Mercian and West Saxon army met them in the town but there was no battle and the Mercians made peace. It was hard to keep any army in the field for too long, as the men had to return to their farms or their crops would rot.

In 869 the Vikings returned to East Anglia and landed in Thetford, Norfolk. The East Anglians resisted this time, not that it did them any good. King Edmund refused to renounce Christianity and became St. Edmund after being shot to death with arrows; his remains were buried on a spot that became Bury St. Edmunds. The *Anglo-Saxon Chronicle* says of Edmund merely that Ivarr "had the victory, and killed the king and conquered all the land," but a late tenth-century book called *Passion of St. Edmund* had the king demanding the Vikings convert, which rather fell on deaf ears, as they tied him to a tree and used him as target practice. According to another account Edmund waited in his hall, unarmed, for Ivarr, and Ivarr had him beaten, whipped, and speared, at which point he was apparently still alive. Then he was beheaded. He was definitely dead at this point.

A legend also grew that his head was discarded but a gray wolf came to where it lay and said "Hic, hic" (here, here). Some people may be skeptical at this point, with a Latin-talking wolf entering the story, especially as the story goes that when the two parts of his torso were finally collected the head miraculously reunited with the torso. The whole St. Edmund martyrdom story was heavily influenced by that of Sebastian, a popular third-century Roman saint who was shot to death with arrows and who often appears half-nude and fashionably thin in highly homoerotic paintings that look like an early version of a Jean-Paul Gaultier advertisement.

Overall it's easy to see why people were not very positive about the Vikings. After their arrival monasteries at Ely, Peterborough, and Huntingdon were leveled, while the nuns at Collingham, just north of Berwick, cut off their own lips and noses to avoid being raped, and were killed instead.[57] Eighty monks were slaughtered at Peterborough cathedral in 870.

After the Danes conquered East Anglia, they followed it with the defeat of Mercia. Its last king, Burgred, went off to Rome on pilgrimage, which was quite common among rulers who were either unpopular or bored with their jobs, but Burgred possibly didn't have much choice in his decision. Sadly he died almost as soon as he reached the Eternal City. Burgred's wife Elswitha fled to Wessex and then Rome but she didn't even make it that far, dying in Pavia. Again a puppet was installed by the Vikings, a man called Ceowulf, dismissed by *The Anglo-Saxon Chronicle* as an "unwise king's thegn."

Still, the imminent disaster did have one positive effect: Burgred and Ethelred of Wessex agreed for the first time that England, or what was left of it, should have the silver penny as a common currency. So there may have been Vikings running around raping everyone in sight, but at least no one had to put up with the nuisance of getting ripped off at the bureau de change.[58]

Only Wessex now remained, and at the end of 870 the Vikings arrived in Reading, inside the last kingdom.

CHAPTER SEVEN

Wessex: The Last Kingdom

The kingdom of the West Saxons was founded in 519 by Cerdic, the leader who supposedly fought Arthur at Badon Hill, although Cerdic is a Celtic name and he may have been half-British himself, if he existed. Until the ninth century Wessex was fairly obscure, noted only for once having a woman in charge, although Queen Seaxburh only lasted one year.

Its most important king was probably Ine, who had come to the throne in 696, and who was possibly behind the creation of the Saxon School in Rome (although it could also have been Offa); also under Ine Southampton, or *Hamwic*, became prominent as a town, although by later standards it was still tiny. Most importantly, Ine also issued laws in 694, the first English codes outside of Kent, which Alfred later cited, and also introduced the first coins in Wessex. The kingdom began to expand across southern England, and during this period Kent was under West Saxon rule, we know, because at one point King Wihtred of Kent had to pay Ine a fine because Ine's brother had been killed by Kentishmen. In the end Ine, presumably fed up with the whole business, abdicated to go to Rome on pilgrimage and stayed there.

Like the other large kingdoms, Wessex was racked by internal conflict. Alfred's grandfather Egbert, who became king in 802, had spent the previous sixteen years trying to seize the crown, living much of it at the court of Charlemagne. There he had seen the steps taken by the emperor to stop raids by the Vikings and after his rival Beorhtric died in 802 Egbert turned up and proclaimed himself king.

Beorhtric had been a sort of pawn of Mercia and made the mistake of marrying the great king Offa's daughter, the "grasping and wicked" Eadburh of Mercia (as Asser called her). According to the Welshman, "As soon as she had won the king's friendship and power throughout almost the entire kingdom, she began to behave like a tyrant after the manner of her father—to loathe every man whom Beorhtric liked, to do all things hateful to God and men, to denounce all those whom she could before the king." She also started poisoning people. Eventually she decided to do away with her husband's right-hand man because she didn't like him, but ended up accidentally killing her husband too. Eadburh then fled to Charlemagne, King of the Franks, and he offered her the choice of marrying him or his son (presumably she hadn't told him the whole truth of why her first marriage ended). She foolishly chose the son, to which the king replied that it was a trick question and "you will have neither him nor me," sending her off to a monastery. But even this didn't end well, and eventually she was caught in debauchery "with a man of her own race," ejected from the nunnery, and "shamefully spent her life in poverty and misery until her death" in Pavia. This is not as implausible as it sounds, as Pavia was on the pilgrimage route to Rome and so lots of English people would have passed through it.

As a result of her behaviour the wives of the kings of Wessex were, uniquely in Europe, not styled queen, nor allowed to sit on the throne, which Asser calls "this perverse and detestable custom, contrary to the practice of all Germanic peoples."

Until the ninth century Wessex had been very much a lesser player in the English scene, and it rose just as Mercia descended into dynastic conflict; in 821 Mercian king Coenwulf died and his son Cynehelm was murdered soon after by a jealous sister. Although early English history is made totally baffling by the sheer number of kings fighting each other, the family troubles in Mercia at the time are slightly easier to understand because everyone in one dynasty had a name beginning with C, and in another rival family they all began with B, another with W, the last with L. In 825 Egbert beat Beornwulf of Mercia at the battle of Ellendum, in what is now Wiltshire, driving the midlanders across the Thames, and he would go onto conquer Kent, Surrey, Sussex, and Essex. Even King Eanred of distant Northumbria paid tribute, after the king of Wessex led an expedition to Dore in south Yorkshire. So in 829 Egbert had become the eighth and last king regarded as *bretwalda* and to celebrate he had coinage minted in London, previously a Mercian city, and the following year he had a pawn instated as an under-king in Mercia, the same year as the Welsh submitted to his rule. When Egbert died, in 839, he was succeeded by his son Ethelwulf without any drama; he was now totally triumphant and absolutely nothing could go wrong.

Ethelwulf is looked on by some historians as being a bit too holy and interested in religion rather than fighting, although the *Chronicle* records that he beat the Vikings at Acleah in Berkshire in 851 and there "made the greatest slaughter of a heathen that we have heard tell of up to the present day" (these reports do tend to get bogged down by superlatives, it should be added).

Ethelwulf had a very religious circle of friends, who would influence his son, among them St. Swithun, bishop of Winchester, a man so humble that he would travel on foot rather than horseback, but to avoid people thinking it was false modesty he would only travel at night. Swithun, who died in 860, is behind the story that rain on his feast day would lead to a typical awful and wet British summer, a tradition that originated on Saturday, July 15, 971, when the saint's body was moved by Bishop Ethelwold from the Old Minster at Winchester to a shrine inside. A storm blew up and it was taken as a sign of his unhappiness; after that it became a superstition that a wet July 15 would be followed by forty days of rain in England (which is often a good bet). Another local bishop, Eahlstan of Sherborne, had helped a young Ethelwulf conquer Kent and seems to have actually led the fighting, which wasn't so unusual for churchmen at the time.

Ethelwulf began his reign with two ambitions, one to make the pilgrimage to Rome and see the relics. The second came from a vision, which he wrote about in a letter to the king of the Franks.[59] In the letter, in which he asks for safe transit through Francia, Ethelwulf tells of a dream in which he is visited by a priest, who was himself visited in his dreams by a man who took him to an unknown kingdom with wonderful buildings. There they entered a beautiful church with boys reading books, and when they had a look at the books the priest found they were written in lines of alternating black ink and blood. When asked what this meant, he was told: "The lines of blood you can see in those books are all the various sins of Christian people, because they are so utterly unwilling to obey the orders and fulfil the precepts in those divines books. These boys now, moving about here and looking as if they are reading, are the souls of the saints who grieve every day over the sins and crimes of Christians and interceded for them so that they may finally be turned to repentance some day." So, to cut a long story short, he went to France on holiday.

This was long into his reign, and by which time he had had six children, who were called, with great originality, Æthelstan, Æthelswith, Æthelbald, Æethelberht, Æthelred, and Alfred; 'athel' means prince or throne-worthy, while the youngest child's name means literally "elf-counsel," elves considered to be very wise creatures.[60]

Æthelswith, the only girl, married King Burgred of Mercia in 853 and was the poor lady who ended up dying in Pavia. The three eldest boys were already fully grown warriors by the time of Ethelwulf's succession, while Ethelred and Alfred were perhaps a great deal younger. (History at this period is so vague that Athelstan may have been from a previous marriage of Ethelwulf, or he may have been his brother.)

After Ethelwulf's wife died the king married a second time, to Judith of Francia, during his trip to France. He was between fifty-five and sixty, she was maybe thirteen or fourteen; it's safe to say it probably wasn't a love match, and Ethelwulf may have been trying to secure Frankish help against possible Viking attacks, which were increasing in number. The marriage came about on the way back from Italy, after Ethelwulf had taken his youngest son on pilgrimage to Rome; this was during a period of increased Viking activity, and historians have considered it a black mark against Ethelwulf's name that he decided to go off travelling. He rather resembles a middle-aged man who leaves his wife to sort out the mortgage and childcare to "discover himself" in Thailand for a few months.

The same year as the Vikings took London, 849, Ethelwulf's youngest had been born some fifty miles west in Wantage, Berkshire, an area so called because it takes it name from Berroc Wood where box trees grow. According to Asser's slightly groveling biography, Alfred's mother Osburh was "a most religious woman, noble in character and noble by birth. She was a daughter of Oslac, King Ethelwulf's famous butler," although butler might have been a more impressive job than it sounds to modern ears, and more like a mini-prime minister. Oslac was supposedly descended from Goths and Jutes who were given the Isle of Wight by Cerdic, and who killed the last few Britons on the island at a place called "Wihtgarabyrig."

Since it wasn't expected that Alfred would ever be king, he was perhaps given a more refined upbringing rather than the usual regal training, which mainly consisted of learning how to stab someone and guffawing loudly while eating a chicken wing. He was encouraged to take an interest in culture, although he possibly didn't fully learn to read until an adult. As a child of ten or so Alfred beat three older brothers in a competition to memorize a book of poetry, at least according to his biography, which was written by someone in his pay. Although the young boy couldn't read, he got someone to recite it to him until he knew it by heart.

Perhaps destined for the Church, he also took two pilgrimages to Rome as a child, a very hazardous route for a young person to go on; rather like taking your kids on holiday to Somalia or the Central African Republic today.

Rome wasn't quite the great city it used to be. By Alfred's time the former metropolis of one million people was down to about 30,000, although in comparison London had only 1,000 people and Wessex's biggest town, Southampton, was tinier still.

The Catholic Church was also going through a troubled period, with numerous popes murdered during a period of intense back-stabbing, even for Vatican standards. In one of the most bizarre episodes Pope Stephen VII had his predecessor Pope Formosus put on trial on charges of perjury and of illegally becoming pope. The trial began in January 897 and Stephen was not remotely put off by the fact that the defendant was dead, and had his corpse brought to the courtroom where it was interrogated while sat in a chair.

"Why didst thou, tempted by ambition, dare to usurp the Apostolic See?" the defendant was asked by the prosecutor.

Silence greeted the courtroom, unsurprisingly really, as the defendant was dead.

The corpse was asked a number of questions but could not persuade the judge of its innocence and was found guilty. Strangely enough the episode rather reduced Pope Stephen's popularity, many of the faithful beginning to suspect he wasn't entirely mentally right for the job, and a few months later he was strangled to death. Popes didn't need to resign back then; among the other pontiffs of the era, John VIII was poisoned and clubbed to death in 882, Leo V was strangled by a rival in 904, and John X died in a dungeon in 928.

Alfred's first trip took place when he was four, and it clearly made a big impression on the boy, who never forgot that Christianity was a link to Mediterranean civilization and everything that came with it—philosophy, law, and most of all, literacy. According to his biography Pope Leo IV anointed Alfred on this first trip, giving him a purple and white cloak and sword to signify he would be king, alongside the honorary title of consul; it's a nice story that suggests ruling was his destiny, but it's probably not true and the Pope merely confirmed him into the faith, for Alfred had three older brothers so it looked very unlikely he would ever have been ruler. It's also suggested by historians that popes were quite generous with handing out these Roman trinkets and titles, which seemed to impress barbarian visitors, but probably weren't that much more significant than a "My dad went to Rome and all I got was this' T-shirt."

At some point in the next two years Alfred's mother died, and aged six he took another trip to Rome in 856, this time with his father, and Ethelwulf married Judith of Francia on October 1. The Frankish royal palace would have been daunting to the Saxon visitors, being hundreds of feet long, protected by round stone towers, walls carved with base reliefs and huge statues, with marble mosaics and gilded furniture (at the time there were no two-story buildings in England, except for Roman ruins).

While Ethelwulf was overseas "a disgraceful episode" took place when his eldest surviving son Ethelbald, along with his bishop Ealhstan and ealdorman Eanwulf, conspired against the king. Together they tried to expel the old man from the land "but God did not allow it to happen, nor would the nobles of the whole of the Saxon land have any part it," as Asser reported. When he returned home Ethelwulf let Ethelbald keep the western half of the kingdom, which Asser describes as an "indescribable forbearance" on the part of the father towards his "iniquitous and grasping son."

Ethelwulf died in 858. A deeply religious man, his will stated that he "enjoined on his successors after him, right up to the final Day of Judgement, that for every ten hides [1200 acres] throughout all his hereditary land one poor man (whether native or foreigner) should be sustained with food, drink and clothing." Ethelwulf's will also included the stipulation that "300 mancuses," a measure of weight of gold, should be taken to Rome for the purchase of oil for lamps in the church to be filed before Easter.

His eldest son Athelstan had been made King of Kent, which meant ruling a small part of Wessex in training for the big job, but he died around 851; at least, he's never mentioned again, so we can presume so. Ethelwulf was therefore replaced by the rather ungrateful Ethelbald in 858, and the new king soon shocked his family with his choice of wife. As Asser writes: "Once King Ethelwulf was dead, Ethelbald, his son, against God's prohibition and Christian dignity, and also contrary to the practice of all pagans, took over his father's marriage-bed and married Judith." To be fair, they were far closer in age than her previous husband (he was probably older) and she had come a long way for a mutually beneficial marriage alliance, and he was single, but for some reason everyone was disapproving.

It didn't work out, for whatever reason, him being dead perhaps one of them, Ethelbald having succumbed after only "two and a half lawless years," as his critic Asser called it, and eventually Judith went back home. While waiting for her father to find her a new husband she eloped with Baldwin, count of Flanders and brother of Frankish king Louis the Stammerer (an understandably nervous man, who eventually got ill and died while on his way to fighting the Vikings). Eventually her father accepted and Judith and Baldwin had two sons, living happily ever after as far as could be possible at the time.

The next brother, Ethelbert, lasted a bit longer, dying in 865, from whatever ghastly malady took people away in the ninth century. He was probably lucky to, for that year the big Viking invasion was launched.

Alfred, meanwhile, had reached the age at which men were expected to become warriors, which he showed to be competent at, although his real desire was learning, not fighting. From an early age Alfred was also very holy, and tormented by his sexual desires. According to Asser, when in "the first flowering of his youth... and when he realized that he was unable to abstain from carnal desire, fearing that he would incur God's disfavour" he prayed that God would send him some mildly discomforting illness to keep his mind pure. After lots of prayer, "When he had done this frequently with great mental devotion, after some time he contracted the disease of piles [haemorrhoids] through God's gift." Thanks, God!

As he spent a lot of time on horseback it can't have been very pleasant. Alfred then prayed to God to take it away, and the haemorrhoids went; however, something much worse came soon enough. In 868, aged nineteen, he was married to a Mercian royal princess, Eahlswith, but on his wedding night, as Asser put it, "another more severe illness seized him" and Alfred was struck down by a severe pain. No one knew what it was, this illness, which lasted for twenty years, and according to Asser, "many, to be sure, alleged that it had happened through the spells and witchcraft of the people around him" or was the work of the devil or "the evil eye"; or, he speculates, it was "the piles" again. Historians think it was probably Crohn's disease, an illness of the lining of the digestive system that causes a lot of pain in the bowels and stomach.

Eventually Alfred went to Cornwall and prayed to St. Neot, a recently dead holy man from the area who was said to have been four feet tall and who had renounced the worldly life to become a hermit. Alfred's malady was cured. He was forty-five by this stage and had the illness for all his adult life, and in fact had just four or so years left to live. Still, better than nothing.

The Vikings struck Wessex in 871, and the West Saxons met them that year at the Battle of Ashdown. Alfred was almost killed because his equally holy brother Ethelred was at prayer and so late to battle, although other accounts portray Alfred as reckless in starting early. The fight was centered on a thorn tree with the two sides moving around it, pushing and jabbing at the enemy; the Saxons were victorious, five Viking earls were killed, and Halfdan retreated to Reading. However just a fortnight after, the Vikings won another battle, at Basing, and King Ethelred died a few weeks later, on Easter Sunday; he may have perished from his wounds, but then it could have been from any one of countless awful diseases people suffered at the time.

And so Alfred succeeded to the throne on April 23, 871, and it would turn out to be a pretty stressful year, with nine battles, eight of which the Danes won. Strictly speaking Alfred had no great right to the throne, as Ethelred had two sons with a better claim; but in the Anglo-Saxon period there was no line of succession as such, only a pool of men considered throne-worthy, *athel*. Alfred had experience of battle and that's what mattered right now, although the people around him can't have been that hopeful by this stage.

His reign started badly; a new Viking force had turned up, the Great Summer Army as it was called, and this combined with Halfdan's forces and defeated Alfred at Wilton in Wiltshire. Alfred paid the Viking leader to leave him alone, a policy often used against pirates and which became popularly known as Danegeld later on; these coins used by Alfred turn up from time to time, with hoards found in such places as Croydon, Gravesend, and under Waterloo Bridge in central London.

In 873 the Vikings established a winter base at Repton in what is now Nottinghamshire, which had once been the Mercian royal mortuary as well as the site of a monastery, although it's believed that a lot of Vikings were buried there along with monks; of the 260 mostly male skeletons at the site, 45 percent have cut wounds to the head. The corpses were placed around a giant, who was apparently nine feet according to the agricultural laborer who discovered it in 1686, before the skeleton was lost.[61] He may have been lying.

Repton is also the last resting place of the Repton Warrior, a corpse that gives us some clue to old-fashioned Viking ideas of masculinity. The Warrior, an unknown man aged between thirty-five and forty-three, had had his genitals cut off after death, quite a common feature of medieval battle, and so the Vikings buried him with a boar's tusk between his legs; they wanted him to have a penis in the eternal bachelor party that is Valhalla. (The Repton Warrior may even be Ivarr, who seems to have died horribly at around this point.)

By 874 the Vikings had fully established their rule in Northumbria, East Anglia, and Mercia, which would have made it easier to subject pressure on what was left of the last Saxon kingdom; the following year the Vikings began settling the land, giving out parts of the north and midlands to supporters, establishing farms, and bringing over women. It might well have looked like the Danes would overrun the Saxons and make England theirs, just as the Saxons had the Britons.

That same year, 875, a Viking warlord called Guthrum mustered an army at Cambridge for another assault on Wessex. However, when he crossed the frontier he was besieged by a West Saxon army, and they only let him go on condition he promised not to invade again. Obviously he didn't keep this promise, despite swearing on the pagan gods, and moved to Exeter, waiting for a Danish fleet to land.

Then in 876 Alfred made peace with the Vikings at Wareham in Dorset but, according to Asser, "practising their usual treachery… And paying no heed to the hostages, the oath and the promise of faith, they broke the treaty" and Guthrum killed all the Saxon hostages Alfred had handed over. To the pagan Vikings, Christian ideas of the rules of war were meaningless, and oaths made to the Christians just foreign gibberish. In contrast Christian leaders seemed to continually demand that Vikings swear oaths or take baptism, even though they repeatedly went back on their word, in the vague hope that one day they'd see the light.

However there did seem to be some divine justice. The Vikings now landed in Exeter, but were blown away in a storm, with as many as 120 ships destroyed, and the loss of 3,600 men. (Again a caveat about figures—that seems like an awful lot of people.)

Despite this, by the end of 877 the situation was desperate for Alfred; the Danes held Exeter and Gloucester, deep inside Wessex, and refused to leave at all, with or without money. On Twelfth Night,

January 6, 878, the invaders launched an attack on Chippenham, where what was left of the royal court was based, and killed almost everyone. The last English king barely escaped with his life, slipping away before Guthrum could find him. It's possible the Danes might have had help from within what was left of the Wessex court, as various noblemen must have assumed Alfred would lose and wanted to be on the winning side.

Alfred fled into the wilderness, to the Isle of Athelney, the last refuge of the Anglo-Saxons, for what was surely the most depressing part of his reign. Much of England is naturally marshland, including large areas of the midlands and southwest, and during the ninth century this part of Somerset was either under water or marshy. Here Alfred and his small band of followers now held out; it was Alfred's lowest point, and although still under thirty he was in poor health and broken by the sheer awfulness of life. This is the period of the most famous story attached to the king: anonymously wandering through the woods, he came to a poor woman's house and was allowed to sit by the fire if he would watch the bread (or cakes). The woman had no idea who he was and assumed he was just some random farmhand her husband had brought in to do odd jobs. Alfred, with his mind understandably on other matters, let the bread burn, and so the poor woman scolded him.

The story is probably fictional, but the moral is clear: Alfred was such a good chap that he accepted the woman's telling him off rather than pointing out that he had more important things to worry about than her bread, such as beating the Vikings. The tale first appeared in the tenth century, soon enough after the event to suggest some plausibility, and what's more, it's the only detailed account of the king that didn't arise from his own PR machine (another tale has him walking into the Viking camp disguised as a traveling minstrel—about as likely as the American president strolling around a Middle Eastern capital with a headscarf, *Team America*-style). At any rate Alfred and the cakes became a popular tale, appearing in

Victorian history books with illustrations showing the serious-minded Englishman trying to concentrate on important worldly matters of state while the woman in the corner blathers away about nothing of importance.

During his darkest moments it was also said that dead saints visited Alfred, among them St. Swithun, whom he would have known as a child. Another story has a poor man turning up and asking for some food; despite his dreadful poverty, Alfred gives him half of what little he has, only for the beggar to reveal himself as none other than seventh-century celebrity saint, Cuthbert of Lindisfarne. Cuthbert was considered so holy that it was believed that anyone who failed to treat his memory with reverence was plagued with madness and "a loathsome stench,"[62] and even the Vikings were wary of desecrating his shrine in Northumbria.

The holy man then repays his generosity by giving Alfred some tactical advice, and telling him that "All Albion is given to you and your sons."

Skeptics might not totally believe that one, but Alfred's attachment to Cuthbert, the most important of the Northumbrian saints, is significant, showing his desire to claim all of the Anglo-Saxons' heritage as his own. He would save not just Wessex, but all of England.

Alfred now had a stroke of luck in his otherwise awful life. Early in 878, while the king was trapped by Guthrum and his men, a group of Saxons under an ealdorman (a leading local landowner) in Devon called Odda were besieged at Countisbury Hill by the terrifying-sounding Viking maniac Ubba. Ubba, one of the three sons of Ragnar, had landed at Lynmouth and saw ealdorman Odda and his men waiting. The West Saxons were mostly farmers and peasants, armed with whatever agricultural implements they could get their hands on, and must have been scared witless at the prospect of what they faced. Before battle Ubba would have flown the raven banner "sacred to Odin, Gallows Lord and All-Father" in battle; it had been woven by his sisters and it was believed it would fly strong before victory but hang limp before an impending defeat, presumably accompanied by a sort of Benny Hill impotence sound effect. The omens were good that day for Ubba—the banner flew. Expecting the Saxons to stay put in expectation of relief, the Danes surrounded them and waited for the English to starve, and were surprised when Odda and his men suddenly stormed down the hill, killing up to 1,200 Danes, including Ubba (usual numbers caveats apply).

And then came Alfred's great Hollywood moment. It was the custom in Anglo-Saxon society that all free men were obliged to bear arms for their lord when it was required, fighting in the *fyrd*, the traditional Anglo-Saxon militia. The *fyrd* dated back to the very earliest Saxon kingdoms, and even after the Norman Conquest the system survived to a large extent.

Over the winter the king had sent his followers around what was left of Wessex to spread the word that all men were to meet at Egbert's Stone in Wiltshire between May 4 and May 10, 878, the seventh week after Easter. And so after months of hiding and isolation and strange visits from dead holy men and being told off by women, Alfred arrived at the spot and saw that the men of Somerset, Wiltshire, and Hampshire had arrived—thousands of them. According to Asser: "When they saw the king, receiving him (not surprisingly) as if one restored to life after suffering such great tribulations, they were filled with immense joy." Cue John Williams soundtrack and, one presumes, a stirring speech by the king.

The crucial fight came on May 12, 878 at Ethandum, an event now known as the Battle of Edington because that's the village where most people think it was. Battle in the early medieval period consisted of two lines of men facing each other, close together in tight formation, protected by a row of shields and desperately trying to stab whatever they could through the holes in the shield wall; behind the front line would have been another lot of men giving support and protecting the flank, like a scrum in a really, really scary game of rugby in which the opposition were trying to knife you in the face. The battle would have been preceded by the drumming of swords on shields, as the men psyched themselves up for the fight; then would come the javelins, followed by the charge.

Asser reports in the *Life of Alfred* that at Edington the Saxons were "fighting ferociously, forming a dense shield-wall against the whole army of the Pagans, and striving long and bravely . . . at last he [Alfred] gained the victory. He overthrew the Pagans with great slaughter, and smiting the fugitives, he pursued them as far as the fortress."

Unfortunately, this being the early Middle Ages, almost nothing else is known of what actually happened, except that a lot of people met very gruesome ends. In many if not most battles of the period we don't even know where the fight took place, so that for the most important battle in English history before 1066, the Battle of Brunanburh, in 937, which led to the unification of England, there are forty different possible locations, anywhere from Merseyside to the Scottish borders. Edington has been located in four different counties.

The battle ended with the surviving Danes surrounded on a hilltop, where after two weeks the starving remnants surrendered. In the treaty that followed Guthrum was forced to hand over a number of hostages, who might well have expected to be killed, since that's what Gurthum would have done, but the king was merciful. "When he had heard their embassy, the king (as is his wont) was moved to compassion and took as many chosen hostages from them as he wanted," Asser said. Christianity was at the heart of everything Alfred did.

Under the terms of the treaty the Danes would keep East Anglia, Northumbria, and the east of Mercia, recognizing Alfred's rule in Wessex and the western part of the midlands. England was therefore split in two, and the Anglo-Saxons, having looked like they were doomed, now controlled everything west of Watling Street, the old Roman road that went from London up to north Wales.

Guthrum also agreed to baptism, with Alfred as the odd choice of godfather (unlikely to receive any birthday cards, except ones with the humorous ditty on the inside: "Have a great party! AND STAY OUT OF MY COUNTRY!"). But this wasn't just because Alfred forced him; to Guthrum's way of thinking Alfred's victory was proof that this Christian God might not be a weakling after all, and could even help him win battles if they maybe went easy on the "blood eagle" shenanigans. The baptism party lasted twelve days, and the English celebrated by drawing another chalk white horse.

Alfred was given respite, and would use it wisely. As it turned out, in 885 Guthrum tried invading again—he just couldn't help himself—but he was easily defeated. This was because in the meantime Alfred had been busy, creating for the first time the infrastructure of a functioning state.

Chapter Eight

The Life of Alfred

Had the last of Ethelwulf's sons just beaten back the Vikings, that would have been impressive enough, but he also had higher aspirations for the country and a vision of civilization. King Alfred established the first national law codes, created an education system, founded a navy, built a network of cities, and set up a national chronicle that would record events from across the country.

Most of what we know about Alfred comes from Asser, who came from a monastery at St. David's in Wales and first visited the king in Sussex some time in 886. How they came to know each other is a mystery but Alfred was obviously impressed and offered him a job; Asser took it on agreement that he could work in England for six months a year and spend the rest in Wales. However, on the way back from Sussex to ask permission from his abbot, he fell ill with a fever and spent a year in Winchester recovering. Eventually he consulted his fellow monks, and Asser's people were fine so long as Alfred helped the Britons in one of their interminable internecine wars, in this case against someone called King Hyfaidd, who made life a misery for everyone around him. Asser took the job in 887; that same year Alfred learned Latin.

The Life was written for a Welsh audience after Asser retired, something we can guess at it because in it he explains the Welsh names for English towns such as Nottingham (Tig Guocobauc). Asser introduces his subject as "Alfred, ruler of all the Christians of the island of Britain, king of the Angles and Saxons" and himself as "Asser, lowest of all the servants of God" who wishes his king "thousand fold prosperity." Clearly it's not a hugely critical biography, and that sort of remains the tone throughout of the tome, which makes Alfred out to be the best person who ever lived. The book ends abruptly, which suggests that either bits of it were lost or Asser died while writing it; or maybe he just gave up and lost heart, thinking no one would be interested in a boring story of how a king beat the Vikings.

Asser was sort of Alfred's PR man and was rewarded handsomely, among his benefits being "an extremely valuable silk cloak and a quantity of incense weighing as much as a stout man."[63] (The definition of a fat man was probably different then.)

Alfred would get Asser to recite to him, until in his twenties he learned to read and later taught himself Latin. Before his reforms Alfred complained that not a single man living south of the Thames could understand the language of the Church, so he took the lead by learning it—by this stage he was in his forties, which was old age at the time.

Alfred's literacy drive was perhaps almost as impressive as his battles against the Vikings. He established an education system of sorts, building schools and re-founding earlier places of learning that had been left derelict; he made local councilors read so that everything could be kept in order. He also established a court school, as the Franks had, to educate the nobility.

Alfred personally translated from Latin to English a number of the most important books he thought it necessary for civilized people to understand; his first effort, which was called simply "the handbook," contained translations of various Latin works, but unfortunately it has since been lost. Among the major texts he turned into English are

Bede's *Ecclesiastical History*; Pope Gregory's *Dialogues* and *Pastoral Care*, a copy of which has "Alfred translated me" in the preface; on top of this he translated Orosius's *Histories against the Pagans*, a fifth century work by a Spanish priest which sought to counter the argument that Rome's decline was due to Christianity (it was a sort of prototype of those polemics which attempt to show history proving the author's prejudices to be right down the years). Perhaps the most significant of Alfred's translations was *The Consolation of Philosophy* by Boethius, a sixth-century lament considered the last great work of antiquity, in which the philosopher reflects on why God allows terrible things to happen and how we should find happiness among the misery. Boethius was a Roman who found himself in prison at the hands of the Goths over some pedantic theological issue, and was eventually executed for it; compared to him, Alfred's life was like that of a regency prince.

King Alfred, like many Englishman through the ages, felt that the country had gone downhill, and looked back at the seventh century as the golden age when kings "not only maintained their peace, morality and authority at home but also extended their territory outside." He may have exaggerated just how good the seventh century really was, but it's true that, with the Vikings having destroyed pretty much every monastery they could find, there had been a decline in literacy as a result.

To counter this Alfred employed lots of people from the continent to aid learning, and also attracted scholars from other parts of Britain. He established two monasteries, one of them at Athelney, and hired "John the Old Saxon" (that is, from "Old" Saxony in Germany) in 885 to be the abbot there. John the Old Saxon may have taught Alfred as a youngster and had a reputation as something of a disciplinarian, and for whatever reason John didn't get on with the priest and deacon there, who were both from Gaul. They, with the help of two other Gallic slaves, hatched a plan to kill him on his way home from church. The idea was to murder the abbot by the altar and dump the body outside the house of a prostitute, so making it look like he was killed while on his way there. A cunning plan—however, in a dramatic twist straight from a 1980s action film, it turned out that John, in the words of Asser, was "a man of customary sharp intelligence . . . and a man with some experience in the martial arts." Although badly wounded, the Old Saxon survived and was able to inform the authorities, and after an investigation all four assailants "underwent a terrible death through various tortures." Another abbot, called John the Scot, was brought over from France in 877, and was stabbed to death by his own pupils with their metal pens.[64]

Trying to encourage as many learned men as possible to settle in Wessex, Alfred summoned "certain luminaries" from as far afield as was possible, among them Grumbald of Gaul and the unfortunately named Werwulf, bishop of Plegum. He remained obsessed with learning throughout his life, and as Asser wrote: "By day or night, whenever he had any opportunity, he used to tell them to read aloud from books in his presence—indeed he could never tolerate being without one or other of them—and accordingly he acquired some acquaintance with almost all books, even though he could not at this point understand anything in the books." Alfred also made all his ealdormen learn to read or else "to relinquish immediately the offices of worldly power that you possess."

Perhaps his greatest achievement was starting the *Anglo-Saxon Chronicle*, a record of events updated annually at five locations around the country, written in the native language so everyone could understand them. These also noted what was known from the time of the first Anglo-Saxon invasions all the way through the Dark Ages, a typical entry being 682: "this year Centwine chased the Britons into the sea." (Centwine was king of Wessex and that line is all we know of his life, except that he eventually abdicated to become a monk.)

No other country in the world had anything vaguely resembling the *Chronicle*, which would last until the mid-twelfth century, written by that stage with increasing sarcasm about the new Norman overlords.

The *Chronicle* charts history back to the time of Christ and records events in Britain since the arrival of Hengest and Horsa, and along the way contain not just a vital record of events but also the oldest piece of English prose,[65] in which King Cynewulf of Wessex is set upon while visiting his mistress in 757 (in the story he fights another warrior, called Cyneheard, and they and all their men end up getting killed). The bulk of the *Chronicle* dealt in misery, a tone they maintain for two and a half centuries, with cheery events such as these:

851 Ealdorman Ceorl, with the men of Devon, fought with heathen men . . . made great slaughter and took the victory . . . They (the Danes) ruined Canterbury, put to flight Brihtwulf the Mercian king and his troops.

870 The Danes killed the king (St. Edmund) and overcame all the land. They destroyed all the churches they came to.

874 They (the Danes) drove the king, Burhred, over the sea; and they overcame all the land.

Without the *Chronicle* and Alfred's other literacy efforts our knowledge of the period would be staggeringly thin.

Western European monarchs were still picking up the pieces of what Roman civilization had left and the best way of recapturing the glories of Rome was through the Catholic Church (the Christian church had not yet formally split between Catholics in the West and Orthodox in the East, but it was on its way). So Alfred made a habit of sending regular embassies to Rome, and in return in 882 Pope Marinus sent Alfred a piece of the True Cross that Jesus died on (one of the more dubious genre of relics of the medieval period—there was by one estimate enough of the True Cross going around to build three ships at one point).

Alfred was also the first king to have a world vision; he made an alliance with the Franks against the Vikings, although the Franks went back on their word and let the Vikings camp on their land; he sent money to the Christian mission in India; the king even became a sort of pen pal with the ruler of Jerusalem.[66]

Alfred, once he had raised money, divided the royal revenue in three. The first went to fighting men "and noble thegn"; that is, the aristocracy. "The second portion he gave to his craftsmen, who were skilled in every earthly craft." And Asser adds that "with a cheerful disposition, he paid out the third portion to foreigners of all races who came to him from places near and far and asked money from him (or even if they did not), to each according to his particular station." This sounds like the sort of policy that wouldn't be very popular today—"let's just hand out money to any random foreigner who turns up"—but Viking-ravaged ninth-century England wasn't a huge destination for travellers or benefit tourists.

In 891, for instance, the *Chronicle* records that "three Irishmen came to King Alfred in a boat without any oars from Ireland, whence they had stolen away because they wished to go on pilgrimage for love of God and cared not where. The boat in which they travelled was made from two and a half hides." Despite this almost comical recklessness they made it across the sea and were able to entertain Alfred's court with their tales, and at the time this would be literally the most exciting thing that would happen at court for years. Ireland was full of adventurous churchmen keen to make harebrained journeys, most famous being St Brendan who assembled a group of fourteen monks to join him on a voyage that landed him on an island "filled with gold fire," which may have been Iceland or the Azores. Brendan was in his seventies or even eighties at the time of this zany adventure.

Eventually the holy Irishmen departed on their mission to reach Jerusalem and no one knows what happened to them; something awful, probably. On another occasion a Norwegian called Ohthere or Ottar visited Alfred's court. He came from near Tromsø, or as he told Alfred "the farthest north of all Norwegians." Ottar was very rich as he possessed over 600 reindeer and some other animals, and told the court how he received tributes from the Saami people, reindeer herders who lived in the north of Scandinavia. He explained how he had traveled up the coast of Norway for four days until the coastline turned south, so reaching the most northerly point of mainland Europe; he then travelled for a further five days and there he met some Finnish peoples.[67] Such adventurousness seems insane. Alfred's court was very multi-national for its day, including "many Franks, Frisians, Gauls, pagan Danes, Welsh, Scots and Britons."[68]

King Alfred also laid down the first national English legal system, a mixture of old Anglo-Saxon customs and Biblical commandments, the "Doom book" as it was called, doom meaning "law." He begins it, naturally, with a preamble explaining his thoughts on the Bible— Alfred never missed a chance to shoehorn in religion—and although in legal terms the code is contradictory in places, it is all based around a philosophy of Christian kingship. In his laws Alfred cited previous kings such as Ethelbert of Kent, Offa, and Ine, in doing so claiming the inheritance of all the Anglo-Saxons.

He declared that no Englishman, however poor, should be outside the law: "Doom very evenly! Do not doom one doom to the rich; another to the poor! Nor doom one doom to your friend; another to your foe." This would be a fundamental principle of English Common Law down the ages, as adopted in the United States and other colonies (even if in practice it's not always true).

In reality the Anglo-Saxons had a system of justice that valued the lives of poor men less than rich; under their legal system *wergild* ("man money") was the value of a man's life, the amount his family had to be compensated if he was killed or injured, depending on social status (the Anglo-Saxon word for man still survives in *werewolf*). Under the wergild system the king was valued at 120 pounds, the same as six thegns or thirty-six peasants, while the Britons, or *Welsh*, were worth half the equivalent status of a Saxon. It was a legacy of the archaic system of justice being meted out by blood vengeance, so that if someone killed your brother, you killed them, after which their brother killed you, and so on and so on for years and decades. In some ways status was more important than social class: a man who was "oath-worthy" could give evidence in court, and to lose this status was devastating.

Since there were no jails, most crime that didn't involve execution consisted of fines or maiming; so that under Alfred's law, fondling the breast of a freewoman brought you a five-shilling fine, leading to ten shillings for sexual assault and sixty shillings for rape. Other blood money payments seem a bit bizarre: it was sixty shillings for a lost nose in a fight, twenty shillings for a big toe, down to one shilling for the nail of the little finger. But if your dog killed someone, you'd only have to pay a six-shilling fine (rising to twelve shillings for the second killing and thirty shillings for the third—after which it must have got a tiny bit suspicious). And while if you accidentally killed a man by felling a tree, you only had to give his family the tree as compensation, which hardly seems a reasonable exchange; the fine for accidentally stabbing a man depended on the angle, which suggested how "accidental" it was.

During the Anglo-Saxon period men were divided up into tithings, groups of ten who were responsible for each other's behavior, so that if one broke the law the others had to bring him to justice; they in turn grouped into bodies of 100, who were responsible for chasing fugitives, in what later became called the *posse comitatus* (and so a "posse" in westerns). They would dispense justice and once a month they would get together and drink lots of beer, so as one historian noted: "Anglo-Saxons at the highest level were accustomed to take decisions of the most serious import at drinking sessions, the frequency of which helps explain why this was such a violent society."[69] The combination of justice and alcohol is always a sensible idea.

Later in the medieval period, when lots of things became associated with Alfred that weren't true, he was seen as inventing that quintessential part of English justice, the jury system; while something resembling it may have been around by 1000 AD, it wasn't until the reign of Henry II (1154–1189) that the jury system was established.

Among his other reforms, Alfred standardized the currency of Wessex and Mercia, and improved its quality; silver content went up from 0 to 20 percent.

The king also wished to increase and improve the ranks of the nobility, which was thin on the ground, so decreed that anyone who had 400 acres of land might become a thegn, the lower aristocracy; likewise any merchant could officially join the upper class if he could show he had travelled abroad three times at his own expense.[70]

Alfred is also supposed to have invented a sort of clock. This came about after he said he would devote eight hours a day to God, eight hours to public business, and eight hours to rest and recreation, a fairly grueling schedule that didn't leave much "me time." Because sundials were a bit shaky as a form of measuring time, he worked out that a candle of twelve pennyweights of wax burned exactly four hours, and he made his chaplains, among them the aforementioned Werwulf, find him seventy-two pennyweights of wax, so six candles could be burned for twenty-four hours. He ordered clergy to keep track of time, and also built lanterns to protect them from the wind (there were no glass windows at the time).

Another impressive legacy was the Alfred Jewel, a two and a half-inch long brooch made of gold and quartz which has "Alfred made me" written on it. It was discovered in 1693 on farmland in Somerset, and now rests in the Ashmolean Museum in Oxford; scholars have debated for centuries what it actually is, but they now seem to agree it was used for pointing at text while reading.

All in all the evidence suggests that King Alfred was a man way ahead of his time, who must have been frustrated by the idiocy around him. Indeed Asser complains that Alfred had to contend with the people's "common foolishness and obstinacy," lamenting "I could mention fortifications ordered by him but not yet begun, or begun too late to be finished."

Alfred achieved all this despite being a total neurotic and hypochondriac, obsessed throughout his life with the idea that he was coming down with a horrible disease or going mad; this may have been related to the torment he felt about his own sexual desires, which he considered sinful. He was constantly anxious about everything, so as his biographer said of him: "What shall I say of his daily concern for the people who live from the Tyrrhenian Sea to the far side of Ireland." As if he didn't have enough problems on his plate without worrying about the Balkans.

It was this mixture of patriotism, social conscience, and sexual neurosis that makes Alfred such a quintessential Englishman.

The Danes attack again, inevitably

The king, just as importantly, made military reforms, among his innovations being the creation of "burhs," or boroughs, cities that were also fortresses. Here large numbers of Anglo-Saxons congregated for security, and these became the first towns in England since the Romans. He was almost certainly influenced by the Franks, who had began to do something similar.

The idea was that no one would be more than fifteen miles from refuge, and it led to the foundation of many towns of importance, among them Warwick, Worcester, Chichester, and Hastings. Some of the burhs were former Roman settlements rebuilt, while others were new altogether. A document surviving from this era, the Burghal Hidage, shows that each town was responsible for being able to feed a certain number of men who could man its wall, depending on its size. So long as everyone could get to a burh in time, they would be safe until the king's army arrived. Alfred also built up his capital Winchester, turning it into something approximating a city, with six miles of cobbled roads, channels alongside each street to supply drinking water to its growing population, and a market selling goods.

It was no longer enough to simply have a militia turning up after the Vikings had arrived and killed everyone; under Alfred's reforms the king's followers were divided into three shifts, so that one-third were always at the royal court ready to fight while the rest were home farming, and were the kingdom to be attacked by Vikings again, he would be able to call on thousands of men. And inevitably they would return.

After the defeat of Guthrum some of the crazier Vikings went off to Francia, led by a warrior called Haesten, the same man who had attacked Italy years back. The Frankish king Louis III chased out the Norsemen at Saucourt, close to the river Somme, in 881, but the following year he died after falling off his horse while chasing a girl he had amorous designs on, a quintessentially French death if ever there was one. Now in 884 some Norsemen returned to England, hanging around East Anglia and making a nuisance of themselves; Alfred sent messages to Guthrum and his followers to help defend the country but heard nothing back from them. Then in 885 the Vikings assembled on the Thames estuary.

The Danes next landed in Kent and took Rochester castle, an important military position for anyone wanting to control the Thames; they were joined by other Vikings in Essex, and soon enough Guthrum went along with the raiders. But England was now better protected, thanks to Alfred, for under his burgh system Wessex had 27,000 men available to defend it at any time. It also had a navy.

The Vikings were preeminent seamen, which was why they were such a menace everywhere from Ireland to Constantinople. To counter this Alfred created a navy, building ships and training men to sail them, and by 910 there were 100 boats in his fleet. Although Victorians saw him as a spiritual father of the Royal Navy this might be exaggerating it a little bit; he did however take a personal hand in designing large ships, and used Greek and Roman technology which he had personally sought out in old books. In subsequent sea battles the English beat the Vikings numerous times, having been bumbling amateurs before.

On this occasion, in 885, the Wessex navy managed to beat a group of Danish ships and take all the booty, but were attacked on the way back; on land Alfred and his son Edward reacted quickly and drove the invaders back east. The new Viking expedition culminated in a fresh peace treaty with Guthrum, in which Alfred expanded Wessex to include the future capital city.

Roman Londinium had been basically deserted since the downfall of the empire. A group called the Middle Saxons had made their settlement a mile west, calling it Lundenwic, before it came under the control of Mercia in the eighth century; now Alfred re-founded the old city "splendidly," as Asser put it in his characteristic unbiased way, with the Roman walls rebuilt. Lundenwic became known as the "old city," or Aldwych—now London's theatre district—while across the river Alfred established a burgh called the "Surrey defense work," or Southwark, which would become the city's seedy underbelly.

This appears to be an important moment when the concept of England came a step closer; Alfred was no longer just king of the West Saxons, for in 886, in the newly rebuilt city of Lundenburh, the *Chronicle* recalls that "all the English people that were not under subjection to the Danes submitted to him." Asser wrote: "All the Angles and Saxons . . . turned willingly to King Alfred and submitted themselves to his lordship." He was, in the eyes of the people, *rex Anglorum*—king of the English. When Alfred made peace with Guthrum, he came with "the councillors of all the English race," according to documents, suggesting he was representing them all; charters from the late 880s now describe Alfred as "king of the Angles and of the Saxons." For the first time, after numerous *bretwalda* who had claimed supremacy, one man did rule what was left of the English nation.

To shore up his power in the midlands, Alfred's daughter Ethelfleda had been married to Ethelred, an ealdorman in Mercia. Alfred fought alongside his son-in-law on several occasions, and gave him a sword worth 3,000 pennies, equivalent to 300 acres of land.

Meanwhile Guthrum seems to have become quite keen on Christianity, and had encouraged conversion among his subjects;

the Danes in East Anglia even started making commemorative coins of St. Edmund, even though it was they who'd killed him only twenty years before. Guthrum died in 890, having become semi-housetrained by that time.[71]

Yet the fighting never really ended. New Vikings turned up—there just seemed to be an endless supply of them. The most threatening was Haesten, who as a young man had joined Ragnar on the voyage to attack Rome and ended up buying slaves from North Africa and bringing them to Ireland; in the name of religious equality his party had also sacked and burned down the mosque at Algeciras in Moorish Spain.

This Viking army returned from Francia in 892, with as many as 250 pirate ships[72] and after they landed in east Kent they were joined by another eighty vessels; Haesten had managed to recruit various random freebooters and criminals along the way. The Viking armies of the 890s were even bigger than those of twenty years earlier, but England was ready.

Before the battle Haesten had sent his two sons for baptism as a statement of his good intent, planning to ignore it afterwards. Alfred and his son-in-law Ethelred stood as godfathers to the boys, perhaps hopeful that this would finally turn the old pirate to God, even though this policy consistently failed every time it was tried.

Despite Danish risings in Northumbria and East Anglia the Vikings were once again defeated, and while Haesten was in the east his two sons were captured in Essex. Haesten might well have expected his children to be at best ransomed or even murdered, and many rulers of the time would have chosen the latter course, indeed seen anything else as weakness; Alfred returned them unharmed, and even sent them away with some presents. He was, after all, the boys' godfather, even though Haesten had absolutely no intention of honoring his baptismal promises. It was a supreme show of mercy.

What was left of the Danish force marched along the river Severn but an English army led by Ethelred was far too organized, and was able to summon men from across the west. The last Danish holdout was at Buttington just inside Wales, where seventy skeletons were discovered in the nineteenth century.

There was now just Haesten's East Anglian army, and in the autumn of 894 the old Viking left his ships to local Danes and marched northwest to Chester, then a ruined old Roman city, but by the spring of 895 they were running out of food. Many of the Vikings now gave up; for some reason one group went on to attack Anarawd ap Rhodri, king of Gwynedd, who had been their ally before. A second bunch of Vikings, led by someone called Sigeferth, fled across the Irish Sea where they attacked some other Vikings in Dublin. Haesten finally gave up in 897 and went to France. He had led a supremely adventurous life, travelling the world and experiencing vastly different cultures and meeting lots of new people, and killing them.

And so Alfred finally had peace and a relatively easier life—for three years, before he died in October 899, short of his fiftieth birthday, having freed his personal servants and his field laborers in his will. The *Chronicle* report that "Here departed Alfred, son of Athulf six nights before All Hallows Mass. He was King over all the English people [*Angel cyn*] except that part which was under the power of the Danes." He was buried in Winchester.

"No man should desire a soft life," Alfred once wrote. He certainly didn't get one.

CHAPTER NINE

The First King of England

W ithin a generation or two Alfred's family took back all the lands under Danish rule, establishing a dynasty whose descendants still rule the country today. His grandson would become the first king of England.

Alfred's marriage to Ealhswith of Mercia produced five surviving children; Ethelfleda and Edward, born between 874 and 877, were followed by Ethelgifu, Ethelweard, and Elfthryth. Of Alfred's wife we know very little—Asser didn't even bother mentioning her.

Elfthryth was married off to Baldwin, the son of Alfred's stepmother Judith, by her third husband "Baldwin of Iron Arm." Most of young Baldwin's time was spent fighting off Vikings, alas, but they were hard to escape at the time; their descendant Matilda would come to marry William the Bastard, Duke of Normandy, and so rule England. Under the terms of Alfred's will his elder son Edward inherited the throne, and Ethelfleda was in effect in joint command of Mercia, while Elfthryth only got three villages in Kent—Lewisham, Woolwich, and Greenwich.

Edward had been fighting Danes from a very young age and so was the natural choice, but Alfred's nephew Ethelwold technically had a better claim than his cousin. So after Edward was chosen Ethelwold went off to the Danelaw where he was proclaimed king in a ham-handed attempt to seize the crown from Alfred's son; it ended in failure and Ethelwold was killed in 903, along with a large number of Danes.

The new king became known to history as Edward the Elder[73] and spent most of his life fighting the Danes. Edward was crowned at a location close to the borders of Mercia, Kent, and Wessex called Kings-Town upon Thames, on the same spot where his father and grandfather has been anointed, and where his son's coronation is still immortalized on a stone. Most of Edward's achievements were in fighting but he did also build an abbey in Winchester and in 903 he buried his mother there.

His sister is perhaps even more important, although widely forgotten. Ethelfleda and her husband Ethelred had run Mercia together and after he died in 912 she effectively ruled the kingdom, continuing Alfred's policy of building burhs all over the country, including Stafford, Warwick, and Runcorn; Wareham, one of the fortifications she constructed, was so effective it was still being used in World War II for anti-tank ditches.[74]

Ethelfleda went on to conquer large parts of Mercia from the Danes, aiding her brother as he gradually annexed all of England below the Humber. She became known as the Lady of the Mercians and was a warrior queen in her own right, taking the east Midlands back from the Danes and successfully invading Wales.

In 907 the Vikings tried to seize Chester, one of Ethelfleda's new burhs and based on the old Roman town, but the English poured boiling beer on them and held out. Then in 910 a great Viking army attacked western Mercia but were slaughtered, with three Danish kings "hastening to the hall of the Infernal One" as the scribes put it. Pushing back, in 917 Ethelfleda conquered Derby, a former Viking stronghold, then Colchester, and then the jarl of Northampton surrendered. By Christmas all the Vikings of East Anglia had pledged "they would do everything as he [Edward] commanded them to do."

Ethelfleda died in 918 and was buried in Gloucester but despite her pivotal role has been largely forgotten by history. After her death the Mercian nobles wanted her daughter as their monarch, but instead Edward took over. Edward had his sister's body removed to Gloucester and her daughter brought to the south, where she was eventually put in a convent.

In fact, from what we know of Alfred's son, he was quite ruthless. Before the old king died Edward had had a liaison with a woman called Edgina, who was either an aristocrat or a shepherdess he had spotted while out hunting, depending on how romantic and/or creepy you like your stories, and the woman became a "noble concubine of [Edward's] youth," according to one description. Soon a son was born.

The boy's name was Athelstan, and he came to be doted on by his grandfather before the old man's death. However his father dumped Edgina when he needed an alliance, and took a new wife, Elflaed, for dynastic reasons, with whom he had several children; Edgina was packed off to a convent and their young son was sent to live with his aunt. However after his sister's death Edward needed a new alliance to win over some of the Vikings, and so Elflaed was also sent off to the nunnery and replaced with Eadgifu, the daughter of Sigehelm, ealdorman of Kent. Edward wasn't going to win any awards for husband or father of the year.

Without a mother, and with his father now married to another woman, Athelstan was raised by his aunt in Mercia and when Edward died in 924 he took the throne, despite Edward having had another thirteen surviving children by two marriages, and his parents not being married. Athelstan was lucky in that his rival claimant, his half-brother Ethelweard, died within a few weeks. This was from natural causes; less natural was the mysterious fate of another half-brother Eadwine, who tried to seize the throne in 933 and who washed up on the coast a few days later having been exiled, although it's unlikely Athelstan actually murdered him.

After Eadwine's death Athelstan felt so bad he set up a monastery at Milton Abbas in Dorset.

Edward had probably nominated Ethelweard to succeed him but it's likely the leading men of Mercia had got together and chosen Athelstan instead; we'll never know, because not only is history written by winners, but in this period the losers couldn't even read. Throughout his reign the new king remained an outsider in Wessex, and we know there were frosty relations with the New Minster at Winchester, guardians of his father's and half-brother's remains.

Athelstan was a great lawmaker who built on his grandfather's work. He abolished the death penalty for children under the age of fifteen for minor offences, which made him something like a barmy liberal for the period, especially as kids that age were executed even in the nineteenth century. Athelstan was also the first lawmaker in England to provide poor relief, his code stating that "If a king's reeve failed to provide, from the rents of the royal demesne, for the poor in the manner prescribed he had to find 30 shillings to be distributed among the poor under the bishop's supervision."[75]

Not that we should get carried away, for the laws of Athelstan also "mention drowning or throwing from a cliff for free women, stoning for male slaves, burning for female slaves . . . In the case of a male slave, sixty and twenty slaves shall go and stone him. And if any of them fails three times to hit him, he shall himself be scourged three times . . . In the case of a female slave who commits an act of theft anywhere except against her master or mistress, sixty and twenty female slaves shall go and bring three logs each and burn that one slave; and they shall pay as many pennies as males slaves would have to pay, or suffer scourging as has been stated above with references to male slaves."[76] Likewise a law from the mid-tenth century describes one widow being sent to the king because she was found with dolls representing her victims and had driven nails into them—she was as a result drowned at London bridge. So it wasn't quite a social democrat paradise.

Of course, what mattered to a king of the tenth century was not reform of the law but great battles, and in 937 Athelstan won a spectacular (but mostly forgotten) victory at Brunanburh, perhaps the most important event in early English history; there a joint army of West Saxon and Mercian soldiers defeated a force of Vikings, Scots, Britons, and various other rabble.

It began when Sithric of York died in 927 and Athelstan immediately took the opportunity to annex the Viking kingdom. The last holdout against the kings of Wessex was the area around York, which was ruled by a succession of Viking maniacs, but in 927 they accepted Athelstan as ruler. July 12, 927, when the whole of Northumbria accepted Athelstan's rule, is the date when the unity of England was formally recognized.

He didn't stop there, marching all the way to northern Scotland to battle King Constantine, after the Scots ruler had failed to acknowledge him as overlord. During his trip he also sacked Bamburgh castle in Northumbria because the local earl, Ealdred Ealdulfing, did not bow to his authority. From 927 to 934 there would be peace in the north, which for the standards of the time was an age.

Viking York had developed a strong and distinctive culture of its own, mixing Scandinavian, Saxon, and Irish influences; although it became an important trading center and produced all sorts of coins of interests to specialists in that area, as well as bone-combs, perhaps the most curious thing found there is the "world's largest human coprolite"—that is, fossilized feces.

Despite promising never to deal with "idol worshippers," in 937 Constantine had gone into alliance with Olaf of York and Owain of Strathclyde (the Welsh-speaking kingdom of western Scotland). They marched south, in direct challenge to Athelstan.

There were very heavy casualties on both sides, but Athelstan's army won, and an Anglo-Saxon poem about the battle states that at the end of the day five young kings lay dead: "Stretched lifeless by the sword, and with them seven of Olaf's earls and a countless host of seamen of Scots." The poem continues: "Never in this island before now, so far as the books of our ancient historians tells us, has an army been put to greater slaughter at the edge of the sword, since the time when the Angles and Saxons made their way hither from the east over the wide seas, invading Britain, when warriors eager for glory, proud forgers of battle, overcame the Britons and won for themselves a country."

The battle was estimated to involve as many as 15,000 on each side, larger than that at Hastings in 1066, and was known at the time as "the great war"; it appears not just in the *Anglo-Saxon Chronicle* but in various Norse, Celtic, and Latin chronicles, and even in the Icelandic sagas.

Today so little is remembered of the great Battle of Brunanburh that there are forty possible locations for the conflict, among them Dumfriesshire, Northumberland, Cheshire, and Wiltshire. Somewhere in Cumbria or maybe Durham seems to be the most likely, although a golf club in Merseyside is still claimed as a location and locals are planning a Viking theme park based on the idea, so let's hope for their sakes they're right.

Where Athelstan did not use violence to conquer Vikings, he used sex. Sithric of York, who had gone by the rather grand title, "King of the Fair Foreigners and the Dark Foreigners," had been married off to one of Athelstan's sisters before his death. Athelstan had nine sisters to marry off in total; when in 929 Henry the Fowler, king of Saxony, asked for a bride for his son Otto, Athelstan sent two of his half-sisters to Germany to let the king choose. How depressing the journey back must have been for the one not picked.

Athelstan in 926 had married his half-sister Ealdhild to Hugh the Great, king of the Franks, and the dowry included not just perfumes, horses, an onyx vase, jewels, and the swords of Constantine and Charlemagne, but the lance that pierced Christ and "a small piece of the holy and wonderful Cross enclosed in Crystal." Athelstan had become something of a player in international politics, giving aid to his godson Alain of Brittany in his fight against Vikings. Alain "of the twisted beard" was so tough he liked to hunt bears with a stick rather than a spear, hitting them over the head.

After his victory in York Athelstan now went by the title *rex Anglorum*, king of the English, on his coins; for the first time in history, one man ruled England. Although the kings of Wessex had united the country, much of it had a very large Danish population, but when Athelstan took over the Danelaw he did not replace the Viking aristocracy; instead those listed as swearing to him were, their names suggest, the sons and grandsons of Danes who had settled in the ninth century. Athelstan did, however, encourage Saxon thegns to buy land in Viking territories to Anglicize them. Otherwise there doesn't seem to have much hurry to assimilate then; Athelstan's nephew King Edgar decreed that the Danes should obey "such good laws as they best prefer."

The Vikings had changed the character of much of the country, the newcomers having built 1,400 towns and villages in the north and east with slightly harsh-sounding names beginning with "Sc" or ending with "by," including Derby, Rugby, Grimsby, Scunthorpe, and Scarborough; today there are 850 places ending in "by," in England, over half of them in Yorkshire of Lincolnshire.

Yet within quite a short time the hostility between Saxons and Danes had softened; while the two groups would live in separate villages at first and presumably try their best to avoid each other, as time went by they began to communicate and, as is inevitable, to intermarry. It certainly helped that the two groups also had a similar language, but they were distinct enough to present communication difficulties, and as a result the neighbors were forced to drop the unnecessary verb endings and pointless cases that make learning most continental languages so difficult, and English became much simpler.

Old English was needlessly complicated before the Vikings arrived; it had three genders, while nouns could be spelled five different ways depending on the case, and adjectives had up to eleven forms. Even "the" was spelled nine ways depending on whether it was masculine, feminine, or neuter, single or plural. Afterward many English words had as few as two different verb endings (I do, you do, he does, etc.), adjectives and nouns were standardized, and gender started to be phased out, a process finished under the Normans (today there are only extremely rare examples, like blond/blonde). That is why today German grammar looks utterly baffling, bordering on torture, to English speakers.

The Danes also added to the richness of our vocabulary, adding such words as *scream, take, clasp, skull, anger, bang, berserk, clasp, cunning, gruesome, hit, rape, screech, scuffle, scream, slaughter, take,* and *skull.*

Of course not all Norse-English words relate to violence, and without them we'd have no *wish* and *want, raise* and *rear, craft* and *skill, they, them,* and *their, big, baffled, build, both, glance, glimmer, gloat, kneel,* or *lift.* Yorkshire dialect in particular, which has given Standard English words such as *dollop, gawp,* and *nay,* is heavily Viking-influenced. In the case of some verbs and nouns, both the Anglo-Saxon and Viking versions survived, eventually to develop subtle differences of meaning. *Craft,* an Anglo-Saxon word, and *skill,* which is Norse, originally had the same definition, and the same goes for *wish* and *want,* or *raise* and *rear.* So the Vikings made English a richer language, although whether the monks having the tops of their heads chopped off at the time would have appreciated this is a moot point.

Athelstan, like his grandfather, was an enlightened Christian monarch. Such was his reputation for learning that poets and scholars came to his court from all over western Christendom, and he was even asked to arbitrate on continental disputes, helping to make Alan Twisted-Beard ruler of Brittany. Other leaders, such as Harold Fine-Hair of Norway, sent their children to be fostered at his court, while Otto of Germany sent him books. He had a great interest in book-collecting and learning that was unusual at the time, and beyond his kingdom he had a reputation for amassing relics.[77] His court included Irish bishops, a Breton soldier, an Icelandic poet, and the greatest continental scholar of his day, Israel the Grammarian.[78]

Athelstan's rule was aimed at 'ensuring that the Christian ideals promoted and discussed at his court found expression in his legislative program and that he governed his united realm as a truly Christian monarch,"[79] and, when he was consecrated by the Archbishop of Canterbury, he became the first king to wear a crown (earlier kings had worn a helmet) as well as a ring, sword, and rod of office. Athelstan was also the first king to have a royal portrait, in which he appears wearing an imperial crown, his hair in ringlets entwined with threads of gold. He's probably the oldest ruler who a time traveller would look at and obviously recognize as a medieval king, as viewed in the popular imagination.

Being a very religious man, he reinvigorated the monastic movement, and was also addressed as *Rex pius Athelstan*, in a poem of that name which called him "Holy King Athelstan, renowned through the wide world"; while others called him "Emperor of the world of Britain," "king of the English," and *monarchus totius Britanniae*.

Having asserted his power over the whole country, Athelstan called national assemblies of bishops and lords for the first time, and divided the Midlands into counties; he was also the first to define by law who got to mint coins across the country, an important aspect of royal authority. England was most certainly now a kingdom. An eleventh-century scribe from Exeter described Athelstan as a "king who ruled England alone which, before him, many kings had held among themselves." One poet, known only as Petrus and living at the time, wrote of him: "Whom he now rules with this Saxonia now made whole: King Athelstan lives glorious through his deeds." When he died in 939 the *Annals of Ulster* noted: "Athelstan king of the English died, the roof tree of the honour of the western world."

And yet not only is his great battle forgotten but the first king of England is largely unknown; his anniversary was barely noted in 1939, although in fairness we had other things to worry about, and if you asked the average person today what they thought of Athelstan, they'd probably guess it was some godforsaken place in central Asia.

This "roof tree of honour of the western world" was famous in the medieval period and was even mentioned in Shakespeare, and it was only from the sixteenth century that Athelstan became increasingly forgotten, as his grandfather became more famous. Perhaps it was because Alfred's narrative of having our backs against the wall is more attractive than Athelstan's story of cementing the legacy, or that Alfred had commissioned a biographer to record his great achievements, and that a series of attractive stories about him fired the imagination. There was, according to some sources, a biography of Athelstan written during his lifetime but it was lost.

The only people who vaguely celebrate Alfred's grandson today are the Freemasons, who trace their origins to King Athelstan, but their interpretation of their own history can be imaginative, to put it kindly.

Athelstan was followed by his half-brother Edmund I, "the deed-doer" (939–946), who may have earned his proactive nickname after defeating the Scots king of Strathclyde, taking his two sons hostage, and having them blinded. Edmund spent most of his time fighting the remaining Vikings of York, and helped to further promote monasteries across the country. A potentially glorious reign was cut short when the king got into a fight with a gatecrasher at a royal party, the brawl ending with king and intruder stabbing each other to death; this wasn't a time of great courtly etiquette and decorum. The unwanted guest, an exiled thief, had threatened one of Edmund's servants, and under the customs of the day the king was expected to step into a fight involving his men. (An alternative, more boring explanation is that he was just assassinated).

He was succeeded by his brother Eadred (946–955), who continued the conquest of Viking York, fighting its ruthless leader Eric Bloodaxe. Eric was a Viking so famously bloodthirsty that he murdered at least two of his own brothers—although he had about twenty to start with—before his untimely end. (Erik also went by the nickname "brother killer" although it should strictly speaking be *"brothers* killer.") Eventually he was killed by another Viking, and York was finally, fully pacified in the 950s, having been Viking for almost a century.

The Norsemen, it seems, were gone for good as a military threat. Eadred then had himself crowned with the rather grand title "King of the Anglo-Saxons, Northumbrians, Pagans, and Britons," before dying of an unknown illness at the age of thirty-two (a pretty good age for the time, at least if you spent your time fighting Vikings). In fact Anglo-Saxon monarchs loved to use quite overblown titles. Athelstan was "King of the Whole of Britain," Edmund was "King of the English and of other peoples governor and director," while Edwig (955–959) was "King by the will of God, Emperor of the Anglo-Saxons and Northumbrians, governor of the pagans, commander of the British" and Edmund's son Edgar styled himself "Autocrat of all Albion and its neighboring realms."

Then came Edmund's reckless sixteen-year-old son Edwig, who caused an outrage by failing to turn up to his own coronation. Bishop Dunstan was so angry that he marched to the king's nearby quarters, where he found the teenager in bed with a "strumpet" and the strumpet's mother. The fact that she was his cousin probably didn't do his case much good. Edwig went on to do the decent thing by marrying the young woman, until the Church decreed that, as she was related, the marriage was illegal.[80]

Dunstan, however, had to flee the country, with the king following him to his monastery in Flanders and plundering it. Luckily for the bishop the excitable young monarch died mysteriously a couple of years later, replaced by his brother Edgar (959–975).[81] Edwig was only eighteen, but had already made himself so unpopular that the kingdom was briefly split, with the north in rebellion (although for a long while the north was generally in rebellion for some reason or other). It was with Edgar that the kingdom of England was finally established; when subsequent kings wanted to affirm their right to rule they would generally cite Edgar's reign as being the time when everything worked. By this time the country was divided into shires and hundreds, or *wapentake* as they were called in the Danelaw, the divisions that made it possible to have a fully functional legal system; these shires, or *counties* as they came to be known after the Norman conquest, became the basic subdivision of government in the English-speaking world.

Edgar was so powerful that he had three coronations, first in Kingston and then towards the end of his reign in Bath and Chester, just to show who was boss; after that he had seven Scots and Welsh kings row him on the River Dee, a medieval equivalent of the Mafia underling bringing the boss a cake. But his coronation, in which for the first time a bishop placed the crown on the king's head, was obviously a winning formula, as his ceremony is pretty much the same as that of Elizabeth II in 1953 (give or a take a few television cameras). With it Alfred's family had finally achieved the unity of England.

CHAPTER TEN

Alfred's Legacy

Alfred wanted the crown handed down "the spear side and not to the spindle side," that is, for the throne to pass through the male line. He got his wish but his male descendants died out in 1126 with Edgar the Atheling, who as a boy in 1066 was unable to challenge the French-speaking Viking William the Conqueror. Alfred's descendants, though, have spread around the globe, but more important is his political legacy, paving the way for English Common Law to be developed in future centuries.

So while Athelstan's star faded in the medieval period, Alfred's rose, and so by the fifteenth century the feeble-minded Henry VI was trying to have him made a saint. This didn't happen, but Alfred is today the only English king to be styled the great, although much of what is recorded of him only became known in Tudor times, partly by accident. Matthew Parker, a sixteenth-century Archbishop of Canterbury with a keen interest in history, published Asser's *Life of Alfred* in 1574, having found the manuscript after the dissolution of the monasteries. Sadly, while copies were made in the meantime, the original *Life* was burned in a famous fire at Ashburnham house in Westminster on October 23, 1731.

The Ashburnham collection had been amassed by Sir Robert Cotton in the late sixteenth and early seventeenth centuries, but much of it was destroyed that day, perhaps the majority of recorded Anglo-Saxon history. Boys from nearby Westminster School had gone into the blaze alongside the owner and his son to rescue manuscripts, but much was lost, among them the only surviving manuscript of *Life of Alfred*, as well as that of *Beowulf*. Luckily Parker had had it printed, even if he had made alterations in his copy that to historians are infuriating because they cannot be sure if they are authentic. We also know that Archbishop Parker was a bit confused, or possibly just a liar; he claimed Alfred had founded his old university, Oxford, which was clearly untrue, and he was probably trying to make his alma mater sound grander than Cambridge. Oxford university dates from the twelfth century, Cambridge a bit later, but in Alfred's time the village of Oxford would have been no more than a few huts.[82] A copy of *Beowulf* had also been made, although the poem only became widely known in the nineteenth century.

The fire also destroyed the oldest copy of the Burghal Hidage, a unique document listing towns of Saxon England and provisions for defense made during the reign of Edward the Elder. An eighth-century illuminated gospel book from Northumbria was also lost.

Alfred's popularity continued to rise in time. Sir John Spelman's version of the *Life* was published in 1642–1643, apparently for the edification of King Charles I, which obviously didn't work, as he ended up being beheaded by his own people. Alfred was among sixteen people included in the Temple of British Worthies, an eighteenth-century feature of Stowe House, Buckinghamshire, one of the great country homes of the period, and one of our only three monarchs. His popularity reached a peak in the eighteenth and nineteenth centuries; when in 1740 the royal court celebrated the accession of Alfred's German descendant George I, Thomas Arne wrote an opera, *Alfred*, about the king who had founded the country (among its seven songs was "Rule Britannia").

Alfred became the epitome of heroic kingship, justice, and liberty, praised in poems by Shelley and Wordsworth; it was partly helped by the fact that we know so little of him, but also that the monarchs of the age seemed the exact opposite. George I, the first of a series of witless, boorish morons to compose the House of Hanover, had been cuckolded by a Swede, who he then had murdered, and had his wife locked in a dungeon for thirty-odd years until her death; the exact opposite of Alfred, in other words. By Wordsworth's time the country was ruled by George III, who was insane, and who was followed by the debauched, grossly obese playboy, the former Prince Regent, now George IV. The upright Victorian period, a reaction to this decadent way of life, therefore idealized Alfred, who was referred to as "England's Darling" in one poem.

Schoolchildren were now taught the story of the king and the cakes as part of national folklore, the king epitomizing everything that was good in the English character. The Victorians especially loved Alfred, considering him to have all the qualities that made a great Englishman: courage, fortitude, learning, sexual weirdness. They marked the millennium anniversary of his death with a ceremony in Winchester in which universities from Britain, America, and the other English-speaking countries put up a statue, raised at the cost of 5,000 pounds. Unfortunately they got the actual year wrong, and this was done in 1901, when he actually died in 899. There was also an exhibition at the British Museum, and among the items on display were passages from the *Anglo-Saxon Chronicle*, a copy of Asser's *Life*, as well as some of the books Alfred translated, and illuminated gospels from the era. There were also some jewels, including two gold rings, one belonging to Ethelwulf, which had been found in Wiltshire in 1780, and picked up by a laborer who sold it for thirty-four shillings. The other had been commissioned by Alfred's sister, Eathelswitha, Queen of Mercia, and bears the title *Eathelswitha Regna;* it was discovered in Yorkshire in the 1870s.

But in the wider scheme of things these trinkets are not important; his lasting legacy is the institutions around us, both in England and those countries that derive their political systems from the Anglo-Saxons. Alfred, having rescued the country from conquest, helped to establish one of the oldest and longest lasting of nation-states, whose inhabitants have been lucky to enjoy stable institutions and the rule of law for most of the time since. He also brought the country's culture back in touch with Europe, spreading literacy and knowledge of the Latin world—for all this it's right to call him the Great.

The 1901 parade also passed into Winchester Cathedral, last resting place of numerous Saxon kings, among them Alfred's father and grandfather, Ethelwulf and Egbert; yet the whereabouts of the bones of England's founder remain a mystery. Edward the Elder had his parents' bodies reinterred at the Minster in Winchester, but in the twelfth century Alfred's Norman descendant Henry I had them reburied in Hyde Abbey. Unfortunately it was destroyed in the Reformation and his remains were lost; the site then became a prison and during rebuilding work all the bones in what had been Hyde Abbey were scattered.

It seems wrong that the man who founded the nation is buried under an old prison in Hampshire rather than under a 300-foot monolith in the center of the capital. However, after the discovery of Richard III's body under a parking lot in Leicester in 2012 there was renewed hope in finding Alfred; Richard's corpse had been lost after the abbey where it was buried was ransacked by religious fanatics (as it happened, the body of Henry I also turned up in 2014 under yet another parking lot, his resting place of Reading Abbey having also been destroyed in the Reformation).

By this stage archaeologists from the University of Winchester had in fact already been analyzing six skeletons found at St Bartholomew's church, built on the site of Hyde Abbey. They looked at some bones discovered in the 1990s and concluded that a hipbone dated to the time of Alfred and probably belonged to a member of his family, most likely Alfred, Edward, or his brother Ethelweard, although unlike in Richard III's case there were no direct male or female descendants to make the match—so perhaps we'll never know.

The search continues, but perhaps it doesn't matter. His real legacy is England, its customs and freedom, a people descended from both Saxons and Vikings under the rule of law. Cuthbert was right: All Albion was given to him and his sons.

Bibliography

This is an introduction to the subject, as the name probably suggests, and far more can be discovered in detail in the following books:

Ackroyd, Peter *Foundation*

Adams, Max *The King in the North*

Albert, Edoardo and Tucker, Katie *In Search of Alfred the Great*

Ashley, Mike *British Kings And Queens*

Brooke, Christopher *The Saxon and Norman Kings*

Brownworth, Lars *Sea Wolves: A History of the Vikings*

Bryson, Bill *Mother Tongue*

Campbell, James (ed) *The Anglo-Saxons*

Clements, Jonathan *Vikings*

Crossley-Holland, Kevin *The Anglo-Saxon World*

Deary, Terry *The Smashing Saxons*

Foot, Sarah *Athelstan*

Fraser, Antonia *The Lives of the Kings and Queens of England*

Frere, Sheppard *Britannia: A History of Roman Britain*

Foot, Sarah *Athelstan: The First King of England*

Hindley, Geoffrey *The Anglo-Saxons: A Brief History*

Higham, Nicholas J, and Ryan, Martin J *The Anglo-Saxon World*

Holland, Tom *Athelstan: The Making of England*

Lees, Beatrice Adelaide *Alfred the Great: The Truth Teller, the Maker of England*

Lacey, Robert Great *Tales from English History (Part One)*

McKilliam, A. E. *The Story of Alfred the Great*
Oliver, Neil *The Vikings: A History*
Ormod, W. M. *The Kings and Queens of England*
Palmer, Alan *Kings and Queens of England*
Parker, Philip *The Northmen's Fury*
Pollard, Justin *Alfred the Great*
Ramirez, Janina *The Private Lives of the Saints*
Schama, Simon *A History of Britain Part One*
Speck, W. A. *A Concise History of Britain*
Stenton, Sir Frank *Anglo-Saxon England*
Stone, Norman: Ed *The Makers of English History*
Strong, Roy *The Story of Britain*
Tombs, Robert *The English and Their History*
White, R. J. *A Short History of England*
Wickham, Christopher *The Inheritance of Rome: A History of Europe from 400 to 1000*
Wood, Michael *In Search of the Dark Ages*

Notes

Introduction

1 Some question whether this was really the first Viking attack on England.

2 Canute (1016–1035) is known as the great in his native Denmark.

3 Robert Tombs. Marcus Aurelius and Alfonso X of Castile are the rulers in question.

Chapter 1

4 Also called *Apocalypse*, it describes a series of catastrophic events featuring a number of alarming figures such as "the Whore of Babylon" and "the Beast." As far back as the fourth century church leaders considered taking it out, as it was so prone to be misinterpreted, while nineteenth-century humanist writer Robert Ingersoll described it as "the insanest of all books."

5 Ackroyd.

6 Ackroyd.

7 A later Anglo-Saxon poem talks of "the city-buildings crumble; the works of the giants decay."

Chapter 2

8 Well, they may have referred to the British Isles, although we cannot be sure.

9 The transition from hunter-gatherer lifestyle to farming almost everywhere led to much worse lives for most people, with a much reduced diet and back-breaking work grinding corn.

10 When the Basque country was part of the French Angevin Empire in the medieval period, the French had a folk legend that the Devil made

a deal with the Basques whereby he could have their souls if he learned their language. After seven years and having only learned three words, Satan gave up.

11 This could also mean "tin land," although no one can be entirely sure.

12 New Albion was the original name given by the English to North America, after Francis Drake had landed in California. Later, following the American Revolution, the British considered calling Canada New Albion, before eventually deciding they didn't like it.

13 The tradition passed down into medieval culture as the Feast of Fools, where for a day the lowest member of a community was given the top job, called Lord of Misrule, but it's possible that it's even older, and that in some pre-Christian cultures the slave was put to death at the end of the party. The custom survives even today, where many companies have am excruciating "fun day" once a year where the bosses serve their employees food.

14 The very oldest Roman settlement in the city is under what is now the office block No.1 Poultry.

15 A statue of her was unveiled in Westminster towards the end of the nineteenth century, featuring an entirely improbable chariot with spikes sticking up. Ironically she had now become a symbol of the British empire, which was far larger than the Roman.

16 Commodus was played by Joaquin Phoenix in *Gladiator*, and he was every bit as bonkers as the film suggests, although Maximus was a fictional character.

17 According to legend Niall found his beautiful wife when a group of his friends were stopped by an old hag guarding a well and had to kiss her for water; only Niall satisfied the crone, after which she turned into a beautiful maiden. They obviously had a loving relationship, for in 2006 geneticists discovered that Niall was so prolific that one in twelve Irishmen are descended from him directly through the male line, and 2 percent of New York men.

Chapter 3

18 Most historians don't think that's how Portsmouth got its name. It's more likely it's from the Portus harbor.

19 Oppenheimer suggests the Anglo-Saxon input could be as low as 5.5 percent, although it is still hotly disputed.

20 Some people think Ambrosius is a different person altogether, though no one can really know.

21 Wood.

22 http://www.ajsefton.com/#!anglo-saxon-calendar/cldp

23 https://twitter.com/katemond/status/661859261887197184

24 Tombs.

25 We think. We can't be entirely sure of what they believed.

26 The actual sources confirming the Saxons did worship the Norse pantheon are not overwhelming, but the likelihood is that they did.

27 This is probably a very simple explanation for something more complicated. The Britons had been Christian, and largely independent from Rome, for some time and probably resented the idea of the religious leader of the Saxons, who had been Christian for about five minutes, being in charge.

Chapter 4

28 *In Search of the Dark Ages.*

29 A sign of how isolated England was comes from the fact that in June 634 Pope Homorius sent a letter of address to Edwin and the Archbishop of Canterbury, unaware that the archbishop had been a fugitive for almost two years and Edwin dead.

30 It has since been used in multiple films, including most recently the 2015 *Macbeth* and *The Last Kingdom*. If you've seen a medieval-y looking castle in any medieval film, it's probably Bamburgh.

31 It most recently featured as the setting for the final scene of *The Force Awakens.*

32 Ramirez

33 For centuries the Anglo-Saxons called the Germans "the Saxons overseas," after which they started referring to continental Germans as Dutch, from Deutsch. When the Netherlands split from Germany in the late Middle Ages this name stuck with England's closer neighbor, while the English started calling their more distant neighbors by the Latin term German. As fans of American Civil War films will know, until relatively late Germans in the United States were called "Dutchmen."

34 Higham and Ryan

35 He was not the only stranger; with him came Hadrian, a North African who became abbot of St. Augustine's Abbey in Canterbury.

36 This is not unique. John the Baptist, if the relics are all genuine, had no fewer than three heads. No wonder the authorities were so scared of him.

37 Tombs

38 Although an Italian called Procopius (500–554), considered the last "ancient" historian, had spoken of the people of the island being called the "Angiloi."

39 It features as the dramatic final spot for the depressing Who rock musical *Quadrophenia*.

40 Hindley

Chapter 5

41 The tribe's name survives in the French word for Germany, Allemagne.

42 This is by no means the oldest customer complaint in history; in the British Museum is a clay tablet from Babylonia dating to around 1750 BC, written from a "Nanni" to someone called Ea-Nasir complaining about the copper ore he had bought. Whether Nanni ever got his copper ore we shall never know.

43 Woods, Michael

Chapter 6

44 Or comes from "Vik," the name of a well-known fjord.

45 Parker

46 According to Clements

47 Parker

48 Clements, Jonathan

49 According to Saxo Gramaticus. From Lars Brownworth

50 Parker, Philip

51 Parker

52 Clement

53 Albert, Eduardo

54 This is a scene borrowed by the TV series *Vikings*, although it is one of Ella's underlings who gets thrown in.

55 Ragnar is, of course, the main character in the television series *Vikings*, which also features other semi-legendary figures such as Bjorn, and Rollo, first ruler of Normandy, as well as historical figures like Egbert and Ethelwulf of Wessex.

56 The death of Aelle by a blood eagle is mentioned in an eleventh-century skaldic poem. As with so many stories of the time, its authenticity is dubious.

57 McKilliam

58 In fact there may have been a currency union from the accession of Berhtwulf of Mercia around 840, and Wessex employ similar coinage and employ same moneyers to strike them.

Chapter 7

59 Reported by Predentius of Troyes in his *Frankish Annals of Bertin*

60 For the sake of easier reading I'll drop the use of Æ from now on, so it doesn't feel like you're reading a fantasy novel; it can be replaced with A or E.

61 Philip Parker

62 In the words of Tom Holland, author of *Athelstan.*

Chapter 8

63 Albert, Edoardo

64 There is some confusion about whether these might actually be the same person.

65 We know that this story is older than the Chronicles in which it features because the structure is more archaic.

66 The Indian story is, admittedly, disputed. It is possible, however.

67 Parker

68 Lees, Beatrice

69 Campbell

70 McKilliam

71 Fans of 1960s British cinema might recall Michael York playing him in the 1969 film *Alfred the Great* during that period when there was a craze for Viking films.

72 McKilliam

Chapter 9

73 He was originally called Edward I but the naming system was restarted after 1066, largely by accident, because there were three Edwards in a row from 1272–1377 and people just got used to referring to them

as Edward I, II, and III to differentiate them. And now it's too late to
change back the system.

74 Woods, Michael

75 Hostettler, John *A History of Criminal Justice in England*

76 The Oxford History of the Laws of England ed, John Hamilton Baker

77 Stanton, Frank *Anglo-Saxon England*

78 Wood, Michael

79 Foot, Sarah

80 This story may be a slight embellishment, but what is known is that
Dunstan and the king's bride and mother-in-law seem to have been at
odds.

81 They were certainly unimaginative with names—ed means "wealthy"
and ethel "royal" or "well"

Chapter 10

82 However, the myth that he founded the university in 886 dated back
to the thirteenth century and was even officially recognized by the
authorities so he may have been genuinely mistaken. People in the past
often assumed things were a lot older than they actually were.